Local Sports Hero:

The Untold Story
of the
University of Kansas Sports
and
Wesley B. Walker

BY

JESSE NEWMAN

authorHOUSE®

AuthorHouse™
1663 Liberty Drive
Bloomington, IN 47403
www.authorhouse.com
Phone: 1-800-839-8640

Published by AuthorHouse 4/24/2012

ISBN: 978-1-4389-9718-6 (e)
ISBN: 978-1-4389-9720-9 (sc)

Library of Congress Control Number: 2009905948

This book is printed on acid-free paper.

Table of Contents

Foreword from Jerry Waugh

I arrived in Lawrence in the summer of 1954 to continue work on my master's degree and to assume a new job as teacher and basketball coach at Lawrence High School. On my way to work, I noticed a young man hanging around the gym, shooting and playing pick-up games. He had exceptional skills as a shooter and in handling the ball. I experienced a small rush thinking this young man might be the cornerstone of my new team. I found his name to be Wesley Walker, a member of last year's senior class---rush over.

The big question was, "Why had I not heard of him?" I had been in the coaching profession for three years; I knew of good teams and their outstanding players. Wesley should have been one of those outstanding players. He possessed exceptional skills; better than any of my players at Emporia who had gone to the state finals that past year.

What crack had he fallen into? Lawrence was moving out of its segregated past. I was a young teacher, and I was not aware of past Lawrence history. How did this excellent basketball player get lost along the way? Could he have played at the collegiate level? Were opportunities not available to him? Why did he not share in these missed opportunities?

We have all missed out on something, sometime. We have often benefited also from shared opportunities that helped us as a community, as a school system, as a teacher, and as striving individuals.

It is human nature to be uneasy with change, but thankfully, Lawrence, the university, and most of us as individuals, have made great strides in racial relations. Is there room for improvement? Certainly. History can make us wiser. Wesley Walker's struggle to achieve is but one example to instruct us about that past, and hopefully, direct us toward a brighter future.

Jerry Waugh

(Jerry Waugh was a KU basketball player from 1947 to 1951, and went on to become a KU coach under Dick Harp from 1956 to 1960.)

Acknowledgements

I received a lot of help from many people getting this manuscript ready. My special thanks and praise goes to Rebecca Altenbernd for taking my thoughts, research, and writings, putting them into better sentence structure. It was she who suggested that footnotes would allow me to make relevant comments without losing my subject matter, thus keeping the flow of my narrative. I kept finding new aspects of the story, and Becca found a place for each one.

The original reason for this story was to have all of Wesley B. Walker's accomplishments in our local history museum, so that in the future anyone could look them up. Wesley had saved all his clippings from early on, so I thought that it would suffice to copy those crumbling mementos and write a few words of explanation. Those few words turned into the manuscript you hold.

When I went to Watkin's History Museum, Helen Krische, the archivist there, was very helpful. She not only saw to the copying of Wesley's clippings, but made sure of his participation in an oral video history lasting about six hours. I also talked to the *Lawrence Journal World* so that they could run a feature about Wesley if they wished. His story needs to be told. My thanks to Helen. The volunteer typist at Watkin's, Nancy Porter, was also helpful, willingly setting aside time to help any time I asked.

A special thank you goes to the reference departments of our local libraries: Lawrence Public Library and Spencer Library. Tara Wenger at Spencer was especially helpful.

A special thanks to Ray Poteet of Alpha & Omega Financial Services for his generosity. Sam C. Miranda (former KU coach 1963-76) was willing to help, but passed away before he could do so.

Also, my thanks go to the many local people who have known Wesley. For example, everyone who generously wrote letters or expressed sincere appreciation for who Wesley is and for his help to them over the years. To my cousin, William Jeltz, who told me about John McLendon's place in my personal history.

A special thank you goes to our local historian, Steve Jansen, who willingly helped to fill in the blanks of local history whenever I called. I thank Max Falkenstein and Larry Hatfield. Also, of course, Jerry Waugh.

Note from the Author

Note from the Author

In writing this story about my cousin, Wesley, I really want to convey to the reader that the era of Jim Crow[1] suppressed so much potential, that we cannot even begin to measure the losses.

---

[1] Ed Abels of the *Outlook* spoke for many Lawrencians concerned about the involvement of "outsiders" sent to Lawrence as part of a "highly organized and carefully directed scheme to stir up trouble in the university and our community" and "to stir up bitterness and hatred." Abels believed that race relations were improving and would continue to do so as long as blacks were "ready and prepared" when opportunities came along. Quoting a "long time resident" ...Abels claimed Lawrence never had "a race problem...until it was stirred up by the University people." ...Although this prevailing attitude tacitly acknowledged the lower socioeconomic status of blacks, it held the black community responsible for creating and maintaining that condition. "Progress depends on the individual and his qualifications," Ed Abels wrote in 1960. There was "no law, prejudice or anything else preventing a Negro" from practicing law or medicine in Lawrence. One only need "make the necessary sacrifice to earn a degree. He cannot qualify in a picket line." The underlying assumption to this reasoning, which had broad support in Lawrence, was that blacks had the same educational, occupational, and social opportunities as whites, which clearly was not true. If African Americans did not take advantage of the chances, the argument went, it was not the fault of the whites. Moreover, even as Abels and others of a like mind tried to distance themselves from race, they constructed social identities based on race and drew clear social boundaries between whites and blacks. This ideology put sole responsibility on African Americans to prove" themselves worthy of American citizenship but left it wholly in the hands of white Americans to decide when blacks had reached that point. (*This Is America?* Pages 48 and 52)

America lost so much in human ability and intellect.[2] Mass fear of a threat to things as they were, caused most Whites to suppress and to deny the most common rights to millions of people (and to even deny their human-ness).[3]

Jim Crow treatment reminds me of how the North American turkey has evolved. At one time, the turkey (*meleagris gallopavo*) was almost chosen, rather than the eagle, as our

---

[2] It is not surprising that the prevailing cultural values of the early New England settlers—free enterprise, thrift, promotion of business, education, and organized religion—are also core values of traditional Republicanism. Religion, ancestry, ethnicity, class, and a sense of place all were key elements in the construction of a dominant narrative in Lawrence that prescribed social boundaries and created social identities for its residents.
Lawrence was contested space since Kansas's organization as a territory and remained so in the twentieth century. Its identity and history, encoded in the rhetoric of freedom and liberty and centered on the free-state/slave-state turmoil of the 1850's, was given new meaning in the 1960s. Lawrence's experiences in the 1960s illustrated the continued struggle in the United States to define and give meaning to freedom, liberty, and equality. The town remained placid as long as these traditional boundaries went unchallenged. When challenges came in the early 1960s, however, conflict was sure to result. (Ibid, Page 22)

[3] I recently came across a footnote in a book that is totally unrelated to sports, which helps explain why our dominant society was so late to accept Blacks in sports: "By no means the least of what the vast wealth creation of the nineteenth century brought about was the beginning of organized and then professional sports. Today, sports are a multibillion-dollar worldwide industry and a major means up the socioeconomic ladder for people of talent, much as the church and the military were in the preindustrial era." (*A Thread Across the Ocean*, footnote, pg. 84)

national bird. He was a noble creature: swift, intelligent, and colorful. He was a wary bird; hunting turkeys was very challenging. Benjamin Franklin said that the eagle was too much a bird of prey, rapacious and loud---not at all how we ought to portray ourselves.

Now consider the domestic turkey. Through selective breeding, we have created a poor creature perfect for the table. It bears no resemblance to Ben Franklin's choice. It has not only lost its color and become a bland white; it is dumb, slow, and soft. All the vigor has been bred out so that it serves our needs, not its own.

Jim Crow sought to make a functioning industry of human beings. It began in 1653, with slavery. The industry discovered that enslaving blacks was convenient in identifying runaways. Efficiency in the trade required total dehumanization. Gone was family, language, religion, culture, customs, even one's name. There was a total erasure of anything marking them as human. Personal development of any sort was suppressed.

To the European, Africa, the Dark Continent, represented the unexplored—ignorance. "Black" stood for evil, in life, literature, or where ever a symbol was needed.

Africa once had a tremendous history: empires and civilizations; developments in sciences, architecture, arts, physiology, languages, medicine, math, metallurgy, and who knows what else. Only now are we beginning to rediscover some of what was lost.

Throughout this work, I have used the word "Negro" rather than "African American" or "Black," because that is what we were called in this period—by polite society, that is. For hundreds of years, we were called the "N" word as a matter of course.[4] That was a slave designation (and therefore by definition, a slur). After slavery, the term hung on in common use for some time. Today, most people know it is an insult. It is a shorthand way to un-human-ize a whole race. Once we were "colored people."

We have now become "people of color" (often to include brown and red skin.) I have deliberately chosen "Negro" since that is what would have been used for Wesley.

Concerning what has been lost to us as a people,[5] the Negro College Fund put it well: "A mind is a terrible thing to waste."

---

[4] Some, especially in the South, just couldn't bring themselves to say "Negro." They would say, "Neg-gra" or even, "Nigg-gra," as if they could not pronounce "Negro," but wished to avoid the public censure of saying the "N" word.

[5] What many people fail to take into account is the loss of legacy wealth that accompanies the loss of civil rights. If, generation after generation, a race is denied insurance, education, and property or business ownership; if survival depends on hand to mouth work and pay, there is no family legacy, no "bootstraps" for anyone to pull oneself up by.

Born Battler

Born Battler

In the major sports, only a few rise to the top, then climb to the next rung to become a champion. Lawrence has had two. Both played in the same 1954-1958 period, and even played with each other. One was, of course, John Hadl. He rose from local high school hero to real stature in KU football, on to the NFL, playing with the San Diego Charger's. Now there is an effort to hopefully get him into the Football Hall of Fame, shrine of the very best. Hadl didn't do it on his own. Way back in Lawrence Junior High School, Coach Duver noticed his potential and later, he was groomed by "Lawrence Ranks High" Al Woolard to become part of Lawrence's long-reigning championship team.

Except for those who played with, or against him, very few in Lawrence today know about our second local sports figure, in spite of his exceptional talent in several venues. That's because he was faced with doing things by himself. In spite of that, he came to outshine all his peers.

His name is Wesley B. Walker. He was just a youngster when he watched a *Movietone* newsreel at the local Varsity movie theater. He was mesmerized by Marcus Haynes and "Goose" Tatum of the Harlem Globe Trotters, who dribbled the ball from every angle and kept it away from the other team. Young Wesley knew that's what he wanted to do.[6] I recall that as a youngster I would see my cousin, Wesley, riding his bike and dribbling his basketball beside himself!

The Journal World articles record his scoring high in the city league, yet he never made the Lawrence schools' basketball teams. Apparently, the coach had little use for this black kid with the "uppity" attitude. He never had a basketball coach. Years later, he played for the *Iowa Ghosts,* and in 1957, he was recruited to play for the *Harlem Jesters*, a farm club for the Harlem Globe Trotters. He played LHS football under Al Woolard, and excelled as a defensive end. In those days, the high school counselor, as a matter of course, always advised Negro students to take the general (occupational) track, not the college curriculum,[7] so

---

[6] When you're a kid, a black kid, the *Harlem Globe Trotters* were like heaven. I watched guys like Andy Johnson, Goose Tatum, and Marques Haynes. To play with those guys? Are you kidding? *(Wilt: Larger Than Life,* page 73)

[7] The fight for control of the black community extended to Lawrence's public schools, which also became sites of cultural and racial struggle in Lawrence. Although the quality of education in Lawrence was generally good, the racism of teachers and white students made the experience for blacks less than ideal. While some black students took college preparatory classes at Lawrence High, others had to plead with school officials who "tracked" or steered, black students away

he never went to KU.[8] Walker, having never heard of things like mentoring and tutoring, probably could not see how he could keep up with university standards.

Walker graduated in 1954. Then he went into the army and his talent was appreciated there, where he was a championship player in football and boxing. Wesley had long boxed in the local area, but in the army, his boxing career took off.[9] He knocked out his first

---

from such courses and into "work training" or vocational training. Karen Byers aspired to be a social worker, but her white advisors warned her how "hard it was for blacks" to enter any profession. (*This Is America, page 98*) Even into the late '50's this continued. I recall my mother coming to school and having a heated discussion with my advisor, Mr. Stewart, to put me into the college prep track, rather than the vocational one.

[8] In exploring the subject of segregation after my first draft, it occurred to me that even if KU was out of their consideration, they might have steered Wesley to one of the eighteen historical Negro universities. I owe a debt of gratitude to Barry Jacobs' new book, *Across the Line,* for helping me to see just how much legal impediments kept Blacks down before 1954 and the Supreme Court ruling in the Topeka Board of Education's suit to save segregation in the schools. (It is too easy to be unaware just how much has changed, since).

[9] In the ARMY:

Boxing: In 1958, Walker fought seven times, knocking out each opponent in the first round. In 1959, he knocked out six opponents in the first round. It took him two rounds to KO two other opponents, but he knocked out eight guys thereafter, to become "the

19

seven opponents in 1958 in the first round, and became known as "The Knock-out King."

A tragic car crash, in March of 1965, would have ended sports for a lesser man. He almost lost his left leg, and would have, except for the intervention of Dr. Penfield Jones, who knew he was a born fighter.

Wesley B. Walker not only fought to save his leg, he went on to become a World Champion from his wheelchair, in both discus and the shot-put. He participated in wheelchair basketball and track. He was the National Champion in the discus and shot- put from 1969 through 1971, and a medalist in the Pan American games. (In 1969 in Argentina, he won the gold, silver, and bronze. In 1971, in Kingston, Jamaica, he won three gold medals for shot-put, discus, and javelin; and was a medalist in the Pan American games). All along he touched peoples' lives.[10] He coached boxing and basketball. When his wheelchair might have stopped him, his

---

Knock-out King." (The first fight he won by a split decision was when he was declared winner of the All-European Tournament).

Track and Field: Having never before thrown a shot, it was Bert John Fowler of Ottawa, Kansas who instructed Walker. He got third place.

passion kept him growing. He went on to a life of service, coaching boxing as well as track and field. He was there for kids, giving them the attention he lacked. What might have happened if back in the 'fifties, things had been different? What if coaches had kept an eye on him when he was young and molded him? [11] What if it had been expected by our schools that Walker would seek higher education? Might he have been a KU star? Might he have become a pro? What might have been accomplished if only ..? What if..,?

Jesse Newman

---

[11] After this was written, I had the privilege of personally interviewing Jerry Waugh on the telephone. Waugh was a KU basketball coach under Harp after Allen retired. He remembered what a good player Wes was. Waugh lamented the problems encountered when traveling with Black players on a team at that time.

What If?

What If?

Wesley B. Walker was born, the third of four sons, in Lawrence, Kansas on May 19, 1935. He attended Pinckney grade school, and graduated Lawrence High School in 1954. His parents were Glen and Alice Walker. Like many Negroes of this era, they struggled in farm/domestic jobs. Living only three generations since the end of (failed) Reconstruction, as Negroes, they were routinely paid much less than their white counterparts (If they were paid at all).[12] Negroes had been defined in the Constitution as three- fifths of a person, and because of slavery, as more of an animal than a human being. Even after the Civil War, when they were supposedly freed, they quickly saw their hopes dashed. Reconstruction in the South was traded for White unity, and Negroes were terrorized into abstaining from voting or office-holding. In Plessey v. Ferguson, the Supreme Court ruled segregation law and "authorities", such as the social scientist Frederich L. Hoffman,[13] furthered segregation.

---

[12]It was not uncommon to be offered leftovers or hand-me-down clothing in lieu o......f the agreed upon wages.

[13] In 1896, Hoffman concluded that abolition of slavery did not demonstrably improve the plight of Negroes. Hoffman was certain that black mortality and black health were a function of the innate racial traits of blacks. Ignoring the recent history of slavery, and seeming oblivious to the social and human costs of segregation, Hoffman assumed that disease

Hoffman's views mirrored the White majority's attitude about the place of the Negro in the social order by providing "national legal sanction" to racial segregation. By 1906, Jim Crow laws and state's rights ruled the nation. Legal starvation as well as economic and educational disadvantage placed the Negro back into pseudo-slavery systems.

Jim Crow replaced slavery. The motive was still subjugation of Blacks. It was put more blatantly in an earlier epoch. Some, (Thomas R. R. Cobb of Georgia and Gov. Henry A. Wise of Virginia to name two), even equated the equality of Whites with subordination of Blacks. A newspaper of 1855, spreading pro-slavery sentiment in Kansas, showed how the thinking went:

The editors of the *Squatter Sovereign* surely shared these sentiments. In a slave society, the paper proclaimed, "color, not

and poverty were a result of racial inferiority, rather than social discrimination or a heritage of bondage. *Race traits and Tendencies of the American Negro,* New York: Published for the American Economic Association by the Macmillan Company in 1896. Reprinted by Lawbook Exchange Ltd. in 2004.

As legal historian, Paul Finkelman notes in the new introduction, "By employing the beguiling methodology of statistical analysis and other tools of the emerging social sciences . . . [Hoffman's book] . . . justified, among other things, massive racial discrimination in the insurance industry."

money marks the class: black is the badge of slavery; white the color of the free man and the white man, however poor [and] whatever his occupation, feels himself a sovereign." Like Cobb, the paper contended that this made slavery the basis for republican equality. The white man in a slave society "looks upon liberty as a privilege of his color, the government peculiarly his own, himself its sovereign. He watches it with the jealous eye of a monarch." The free white man is "proud of his freedom" and "jealous of his privilege." Such a man is "will resist every attempt to rob him of his dominion."[14]

When Walker was born, Jim Crow laws and segregation systems were a way of life for every American, Negro or White. So, it is remarkable to see the spirit of individualism (seen by most Whites as "uppity") burn in the body and mind of Wesley Walker.

What causes certain people to rise above circumstances and say, "I am somebody!" and "I'm going to be somebody!"? This striving to change through practice, pain, and just plain hard work makes him stand out from others. (The ancient Greeks idolized character, strength, and skill as the making of a god. We

---

[14] *Kansas and the West: New Perspectives,* (p.144)

are not quite as fanatic, but we greatly admire those qualities).

Growing from a child to a boy, then a man, the chiseling, the sculpting, of his mind and body came to show itself through sports. As my mother used to say, "We are all born equal, but after that, we have to BECOME unequal." Wesley Walker was only six feet tall, 175 pounds, but his determination, skill, and speed made up for his size. Winning is in America's national character. Notice what sports columnist Earl Morey said about Walker being a winner, in his column, *Strictly Personal*, on April 7, 1964:[15]

> Wesley Walker of Lawrence continues to amaze me. He's retired two or three times from the amateur boxing ranks in order to coach and train younger fighters. But it seems something always comes up that causes Wes to crawl back into the ring, and each time he does, he enjoys success.
>
> After Walker won the Kansas City Golden Gloves light heavyweight title, he "hung up the gloves." But he returned to challenge Kansas University's Ron Marsh in the finals of the heavyweight division last year, and forced the much-younger Ron to the limit before a close decision.
>
> Again Walker quit as an active fighter and went to work building a team for the Lawrence Boxing Club, under the sponsorship of the Lions Club. But when he

---

[15] *Lawrence Journal World*

recently took a pair of fighters to Springfield, Missouri, for matches, it was Wesley who had to take on one of Joplin's top heavies because another fighter failed to show. Wesley whipped the man easily.

Now he's won the Regional AAU heavyweight title and is in Las Vegas, Nev., trying for a berth in the Olympic trials which follow in New York. And you know something?

Wes just might get the job done at both places. Don't bet against this battler.

Walker accomplished, as they used to boom on *Wide World of Sports* in early TV, the "thrill of victory" and the "agony of defeat" by never giving up.

His story has lain hidden from Lawrence history, but through his character, he made his mark on many people[16]. We are lucky to have these newspaper articles and clippings. Without those old

---

[16]For example, in the fall of 1963, in the early hours of a cold morning, Walker witnessed an attack on Leo Bierman, a disabled little person who was universally admired for what he had accomplished despite his handicap. Bierman became a fixture on Lawrence sidewalks, selling pencils from his tiny homemade wagon or driving a specially adapted tractor. Walker rescued Leo from the assault, and held his attacker for the police. The community was delighted. Jack Mitchell later sponsored a trophy for Walker's boxing club. Wesley said it was only after the assault incident that he felt really accepted by the White community.

clippings recording Walker's life-long achievements, this story would not have been told to the public.

Before His Time

Before His Time

In the very year (1935) that Walker was born in his home on the four-hundred block of Alabama Street, only two blocks away, at 809 West 6th Street, a young Negro was breaking new ground. His name was John B. McLendon. He was the first Negro to enroll at KU in physical education. As part of his requirements to graduate, he had to pass swim classes. Thus Robinson gym was desegregated (they drained the pool the first few times he swam[17]); however, the Lawrence municipal pool remained segregated for another three and a half decades.

Basketball was considered a "thinking man's game,"[18] unsuited to Negroes. Then in the Berlin Olympics of 1936, Jesse Owens won

---

[17] Until then, it had been customary in Robinson to allow Negroes to swim only on the last day of the month. "Later that day, the pool would be drained and then refilled for the enjoyment of the white students." (*Embattled Lawrence,* page 145, William M. Tuttle Jr. chapter).

[18] The great University of Kentucky head coach, Adolph Ruff, glibly voiced this commonly held opinion: "Basketball is a thinking man's game, and the Negro is not capable of thinking, let alone of succeeding." (Adolph Ruff, *The Secret Game,* ESPN documentary, 2008.) Interestingly, the first time an all-Black team (the University of Texas, El Paso) played an all-White one (Ruff's Kentucky Wildcats), in the NCAA championship of 1966, Texas won 72 to 65 over Kentucky.

gold medals in the 100 and 200 yard dashes. That showed that Negroes were faster than Whites, (in short distances that is, not in long distances). The distance myth was shattered in the Mexico Olympics of 1968, when Jim Ryan lost to Kip Keino in the 1500 meters. Keino won gold in that one and silver in the 5000 meters, and Benjamin Kogo took silver in the Steeplechase. After that, many Negroes played on high school and university football teams, (since football is a violent, "collision" sport---one of power and speed).

So, the LHS football team was integrated. After all, it was reasoned, the fast, violent sport was well suited to Negroes. Basketball would be a different matter. Since basketball was considered a thinking man's game, it was a very slow process to bring Negroes into basketball.

Lawrence kept its basketball segregated, relegating Negroes to an after-school program with donated, hand-me-down uniforms. They were called the *Promoters*. On 2/20/2000 the *Lawrence Journal World* featured an article about the *Promoters*. My dad, Jesse Newman played center on that team in 1930-33. The team lasted until 1949 when LHS was finally integrated. The first Negro on the LHS basketball team was Leonard Monroe, in 1950. He made the team, but did not play. The next year Wayman Wilburn actually played. Both Monroe and Wayman were former *Promoters*. The *Promoters* were co-champions of the Kansas-Missouri Athletic Association (page 4).

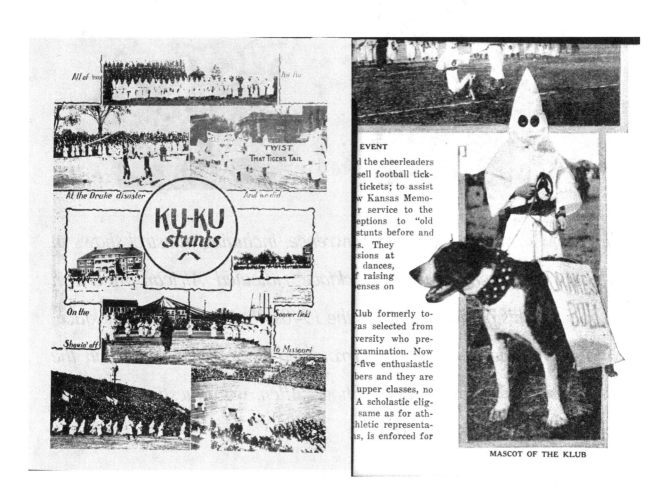

At the Drake disaster   And we did

All of 'em   Ku Ku

TWIST THAT TIGERS TAIL

KU-KU stunts

On the   Sooner field

Showin' off   to Missouri

EVENT

...d the cheerleaders
...sell football tick-
...tickets; to assist
...w Kansas Memo-
...r service to the
...eptions to "old
...stunts before and
...s. They
...sions at
...dances,
...f raising
...enses on

...Klub formerly to-
...as selected from
...versity who pre-
...examination. Now
...y-five enthusiastic
...bers and they are
...upper classes, no
...A scholastic elig-
...same as for ath-
...hletic representa-
...s, is enforced for

MASCOT OF THE KLUB

Jim Crow took many forms in Lawrence, including minstrel shows in which white men wearing blackface ridiculed African American people. In this photograph from the 1940s, the four men in blackface, who played the "end men," surrounded "Mr. Interlocutor" in the white suit, played by Forrest "Phog" Allen, who questioned the end men, eliciting buffoonish answers.

The LHS coach, Fred Noll, coached the team, (after school hours), until 1936. My cousin, Will Jeltz, remembers John McLendon as a student coach for Lincoln Grade School (a segregated school) and Lawrence Junior High under "Dad" Perry in 1934-36.[19] We know McLendon also worked with Fred Noll coaching the *Promoters* while attending KU. His biography lists LHS in his credits for 1934-36. He learned directly from Naismith, the inventor of basketball while a student at KU. (He was the first Negro to graduate in physical education).

Because Naismith was from Canada, and did not grow up with Jim Crow bigotry,[20] we do not know how much influence that had on Lawrence basketball. We do know that Naismith was a mentor and teacher to McLendon, who went on to an outstanding career in

---

[19] William Jeltz is a relative on my mother's side. He told me that McLendon married his half-sister Alice while McLendon was in Lawrence.

[20] Growing up in Canada was very different from growing up in the U.S. with Jim Crow. Phog Allen was at KU during the era that saw K.K.K. events on campus! Quoting from a caption under photos of fully robed Klansmen at KU:

> By the 1920's, Lawrence's abolitionist heritage was under assault by a revived Ku Klux Klan. In fact, in 1924 the KKK held its statewide convention in downtown Lawrence. On the KU campus, a new pep club emerged calling itself the "Ku Ku Klan" (later renamed the "Ku Ku Klub"). On football Saturdays, the Ku Ku Klub marched across campus in klan sheets and hoods, at Memorial Stadium, its members sold programs and "put on stunts" between halves. (*Embattled Lawrence*, page 145, William M. Tuttle Jr. chapter).

coaching basketball[21], the first coach in history to coach three consecutive national titles. (And a Negro at that!) He guided Tennessee State to the NAIA championships in 1957, 1958, and 1959. He was the first Negro to coach pro basketball. He coached in the NIBL, the ABL, and the ABA. McLendon was the best Negro basketball coach, ever, and the author of two books about his fast-break approach. On March 3, 1979, he was enshrined into the Naismith Memorial Basketball Hall of Fame.

LaVanne Squires of Wichita, Kansas was recruited by Phog Allen (only because, according to Max Falkenstein[22], Kansas State University had recruited Gene "the Jet" Wilson in 1952, the first Negro player in Big Seven basketball). Squires became KU's first Negro basketball player.[23] Maurice King replaced LaVanne Squires as KU's next good ball handler in 1955, and would be on the starting team with Wilt Chamberlain. Maurice "Pancho" King and Wes played on a Kansas City team called *Peck's Bad Boys*. "Pancho" was

---

[21] Yet, he was unsuccessful in efforts to desegregate KU's basketball and football teams. The segregation continued until 1952! (*Ninety Years of Struggle and Success*, page 68)

[22] "Wilson did so well, no one could touch him, he ran circles around everybody." Max said that Phog Allen's philosophy was that "If Kansas State has a Jew or Negro, or whatever; we will have to match it." (KU wanted the benefit of Negro players, and probably did not want to be lumped with the South's teams as racist after the Supreme Court decision of 1954).

[23] Walker graduated high school the same year (1954) that LaVanne Squires graduated KU.

his nickname to most of us. Many times he told me that Wes was the best player on the team. We all knew it, so others should have known it, too. Since Allen was looking for excellent ball handlers at the time, what if he had recruited Walker? Right in his own back yard! ! ! What if. . . ? ?

The Good Samaritan

The Good Samaritan

The night of September 28, 1963, Walker and a companion witnessed what he at first thought was merely a couple of vagrants seeking to break into a car for shelter. The two ran when they heard Walker. Then he saw what he thought was an old blanket on the ground. Upon closer inspection, it tuned out to be a pool of blood with what looked like half a body in the center. It was the tiny body of Leo Bierman, badly beaten.

Walker was outraged. He took out after the culprits and picking up one by the collar slammed him to the ground. The man yelped for the other person (a woman) to run. Well, Walker knew that a Black man couldn't chase a White woman-(and at night, too!)

He held the man (Wayne Knackstedt) for the police. They later caught the woman, and both went to prison. Leo was in the hospital, and then he was taken in by a local minister's family for a while, for which he was forever grateful, having been pretty much abandoned by his own family. After the assault he was almost blind and totally deaf.

Most people really liked Leo Bierman. He was always friendly, and he made the most of being handicapped when there were few social services anywhere for the handicapped. He walked with the aid of a tiny homemade wagon, and he drove a tractor that was specially adapted for him. He sold pencils in the downtown and evidently he camped out at night in the car dealership and Goodyear tire place on 9th and New Hampshire Streets, which has since been walled in and renovated into restaurant spaces.

Wesley was something of a local hero. He told me that people were nicer to him after that. He had no trouble starting his boxing club. He said that Coach Jack Mitchell even sponsored a trophy for the club.

Epilogue

Epilogue

Writing this book has been a real discovery. First to discover just how great my cousin is: What began as a tribute for local history has become a deeper journey of personal discovery. I have generally just ignored slights and insults as a problem the other person has, not fully connecting the action with racism. As a result, I was often oblivious to the implication. Who would have thought that the University of Kansas, an institution meant to elevate the mind, would have had in place for generations, institutional prohibitions designed specifically to hold back people of color? I wouldn't have. Yet, in some classes, there was a time when no Black person could get a grade higher than a "C,"[24] a "gentlemen's agreement" kept sports segregated[25] and

---

[24] *Colored Students and Graduates of KU*, (Thesis), 1909, p. 244

[25] *Ninety Years of Struggle and Success.* This policy supposedly ended in 1947, however Kendrick points out that it didn't:

> On May 13, 1947, Malott [KU's Chancellor then] reluctantly signed Bill No. 16, along with three petitions submitted by ASC that demanded an end to the "gentlemen's agreement" in athletics and other extra-curricular activities on campus. Malott's hesitancy stemmed from his belief that the University did not discriminate racially, and that the legislation seemed "directed toward an evil, which does not exist."
>
> Six days later, two African American baseball players, one of whom had played on a team in St. Louis and the other in the armed forces, tested this policy, but were turned away from tryouts. An article ran in the *University Daily Kansan* about what had happened. Coach Vic Bradford defended that "any player that really demonstrated the ability we need for conference competition stayed on the squad." It did not end there, however, because the

Black students in back of the classroom, and denied them the use of facilities; THE GREAT BASKETBALL COACH, Forest "Phog" Allen was a die-hard segregationist; and people in the community gave Black students a hard time as a matter of course.

Who would have believed that the FREE STATE of Kansas was

---

next day CORE, ASC, YMCA, and YWCA protested the ban on Black participation in intercollegiate and intramural athletics. When Paul Sims and Cecil Browder (class of 1950) had attempted to try out for basketball, "Phog" Allen suggested "they try out for the track squad as that didn't require as much body contact." Then when Browder did try out for basketball Allen told him "the practice was only for those men who had been on last winter's varsity." (Ibid, p. 140.) Actually, Allen had voiced his true feelings back in the 20's, as KU's head of athletics, proclaiming that "no colored man will ever have a chance as long as he [Allen] is there." (*Embattled Lawrence*, (page 145, William M. Tuttle, Jr. chapter). In *Across the Line*, Jacobs points out how intimate the game was:

The adjustment was complicated for basketball players because, as desegregation unfolded, they were more likely to bear the brunt of doubt and hostility. "There's no hiding a basketball player," says Wendell Hudson, the Alabama pioneer. "You know who they are. You know where they're from. You know what color they are." Basketball is easily the most intimate of major team sports. Games occur in enclosed spaces packed with fans. Players wear no obscuring helmets, pads, or long sleeves; uniforms are little more than glamorized underwear. "One can see muscles flexing and faces contorting in concentration or frustration," said the 1973 Ole Miss yearbook. "The players aren't little blobs of color that are glimpsed occasionally from the vantage point of Section A, row 43, seat 15, student section, please don't spit on the band, but are actual, honest-to-god, real-life people who are recognizable as such." (P. xvii.)

really a proud Jim Crow state? I would not have, although I should have gotten a hint from one of my earliest memories that gave me nightmares for years: without warning I found myself under a big white man, who had brought me down off my tricycle by the scruff of my neck and was shaking me, his fist rolled up, loudly threatening to kill me. On the walk in front of my house! I had done something "uppity" I guess, although I never knew what.[26]

The irony is that my cousin might have been a hometown boy who would have done them proud. Just imagine if Allen had recruited my cousin *with* Wilt Chamberlain. All who saw Wesley play agree: John Hadl, Bob Altenbernd, Larry Hatfield,

---

[26] After my first draft of this manuscript, I picked up Barry Jacobs" book, *Across the Line*. He covered college basketball and was a sports writer for the *New York Times* for over twenty years. I found his introduction really good. In fact, I quote from it extensively here. I went back and put into my manuscript appropriate references from his book. For example, Jacobs covers the history of Jim Crow in sports as well as the nation. Jacobs quotes Leon Litwack:
"In 1910, in the estimation of a visitor [to the South], race relations in the South had become a 'state of war.'" Leon Litwack notes in *trouble In Mind*, a masterful book on the segregated South. "This 'war' black men and women were clearly losing; indeed, it had become a virtual rout. The other side owned the land, the law, the police, the courts, the government, the armed services, and the press. The political system denied blacks a voice; the educational system denied them equal access and adequate resources; popular culture mocked their lives and aspirations; the economic system left them little room for ambition or hope; and the law and the courts functioned at every level to protect, reinforce and deepen their political powerlessness, economic dependence, and social degradation."

Ralph King, and many others, that Wesley was an exceptional player. What might good coaching have added? KU sports would have been electric! Allen would have gotten even more national attention. He could have been seen as a great figure in the civil rights movement. He could have been on the right side of history. Sad.

We know from Wilt's biography that the unusually tall, talented high schooler was brought to Allen's attention by KU sports information director, Don Pierce, and by B. H. Born, the Kansas All-American "almost run off the court by Wilt in the summer of 1954 in the Catskills."[27] So, the question is: Did pierce know about Wesley? Wesley was scoring big in city leagues. Chances are that Pierce did not follow non-collegiate sports. But what about Allen? Three things worked against Wesley here: First, Allen was a segregationist under the powerful influence of Jim Crow, who refused to even consider Black talent until forced.[28] Second, Wesley was not in high school basketball, only city league and intra-mural play. Third, although tall enough by the standards of the day, my cousin was not the kind of tall that had sports directors taking notice. Allen was responding to outside pressure to bring in Blacks after 1954. He had his own agenda to keep the game "pure." He would see no reason to scout out local

---

[27] *Wilt: Larger than Life,* by Robert Cherry, page 36.
[28] In the 1930's, Kansas University still abided by the "gentlemen's agreement." KU would continue this exclusionary policy in team sports for almost forty years until 1952, the beginning of the civil rights movement, when LaVanne Squires became the first African American on the basketball team. Randolph had heard Allen swear "there would never be a Black in football or basketball….they couldn't even try out for it." And McLendon had attempted unsuccessfully to desegregate the basketball and football teams by trying out. *Ninety Years of Struggle and Success: African-American History at the University of Kansas,* by Amber Regan Kendrick, 2004.

Black talent. To him Wesley would have been invisible.

Allen was a segregationist, and I find it a paradox that he wanted Wilt to play at KU. In a telephone interview[29] Steve Jansen points out that six foot ten inch George Mikan of DePaul, six foot nine inch Clyde Lovellette of the University of Kansas, and seven foot Bob Kurland[30] of Oklahoma A&M (later Oklahoma State) were impacting the game, (in both offense and defense), and that Allen wanted to counter height advantage by hiking up the basket.[31] He wanted to keep what he considered "structured fairness." That was Allen's pet project.

In Allen's day, basketball was a totally different game from what we see today. It was a "slow down" game. That is, the objective, rather than high scoring, was good ball handling and passing. The idea was to have more of a defensive than an offensive game, to keep the other team mentally off-balance. The winningest team would pass the ball in and around their opponent's defense, waiting for just the right shot. Then they would move in for the "high percentage" shot. Most games had a low score. (Coach Hank Iva of Oklahoma held his scores down to under 20 to 25 points per game for many years.) The idea was to create mental tension in an opponent's mind. The shot, when it came, would be either a lay-up, two hand set shot, or a bank shot off the backboard. Then the higher score would be maintained by holding the ball and, by deft handling and passing, to confuse and frustrate the opposing players. This all

---

[29] Nov, 6, 2008.

[30] In 1946, Max Falkenstein broadcast an NCAA championship game for the first time. It was October 3, on WREN; KU vs. Oklahoma A & M; score: 31-3. He became the legendary Voice of the Jayhawks.

[31] In fact, Allen had installed two twelve foot high baskets in a third floor gymnasium in Robinson. (Larry Hatfield, personal interview, Nov. 10, 2008).

changed with taller player who could make jump shots. The fans became more and more intolerant of a "keep-away" game, so that in 1985, a new rule was introduced. It was the 45 second clock, which made it necessary to shoot the ball, rather than hold onto it. Then in 1993, the game was further speeded up with the 35 second clock.

Early on, Allen began to notice that strategy was being replaced by natural aptitude. Allen wanted to eliminate height advantage totally. But he was also a realist who knew KU needed to recruit the best players to keep its prominent place in college sports. A couple of years after Wilt Chamberlain was brought to Allen's attention, he began a full court press to bring him to KU.

In Robert Cherry's biography of Wilt, he describes what that entailed:

> But it wasn't until the winter of 1955 that Allen began to recruit Wilt and actually saw him play. Allen flew to Philadelphia in January 1955 and attended the Overbrook-Germantown game. That evening Wilt received a local award as "the outstanding scholastic athlete in Philadelphia." Coach Cecil Morenson recaptured the event: "Phog Allen came to the Cliveden Award Banquet and introduced himself to me. Then he sat down with Wilt's mother and he *schmoozed* her. And she loved him."

KU sent plane tickets, so Wilt and his coach took a trip to Lawrence. Even though the plane came in at 3:00 on a cold Kansas morning, there were about 50 people waiting. Allen recruited a lineup of "distinguished Kansas citizens, black and white, to win Wilt's heart for the university."[32]

The thing that was most appealing, perhaps, was that Wilt

---

[32] Ibid. pages. 36, 37.

looked forward to being coached by one of the winningest coaches in history. "Allen won or shared 24 conference championships in his 39 years at Kansas. He helped to found the National Basketball Coaches Association, was the driving force behind the decision to include basketball as an Olympic event in 1936, and had helped to coach the United States Olympic team to a gold medal in 1952."[33]

But Chamberlain being coached by Allen was not to be. Allen was forced to retire before he ever coached the star athlete.

The irony is that it was Wilt who ended up really changing basketball:
NEW RULES
(NCAA)

1. No goal tending: (taking the ball off the rim or backboard on the way down.)

2. When shooting a free-throw, remain at the line until the ball hits the back-board or rim.

3. The narrow lane (key) was widened to put the tall players
farther from the goal.

Wilt's influence went beyond rule changes. He changed basketball forever. After Wilt, the game changed from a game without stature, sort of a place-holder between football and baseball,[34] to a true multi-billion dollar industry. Not merely did Wilt and other exceptional talents produce growing salaries, but also growing audience interest, which was to produce in turn,

---

[33] Ibid, pg. 37.
[34] *Across the Line*, page xvi.

huge television contracts, and eventually ESPN.

After this was written, I had the privilege of personally interviewing Jerry Waugh on the telephone. Waugh was a KU basketball coach under Harp after Allen retired. He remembered what a good player Wes was. He said things were different back then. As with so many, he said that he never realized what was going on with the color line. "I never even thought about it." But Waugh lamented the problems encountered when traveling with Black players on a team at that time. He said that LaVanne Squires was a "good" player, "not, in my opinion a great one. Now, Wes was a great one! I remember that he had great ball handling skills."

When I asked about Wesley and Wilt playing together, Coach Waugh made a low, appreciative sound, "Oh-h-h-h, that would have been *really great*!"

Walker's Statistics

Walker's Statistics

Golden Gloves, Light Heavyweight

1955-Topeka Novice Champion
1956-Kansas City Kansas Open Champion
1957-Kansas City Kansas Open Champion
1956-Kansas City Kansas Open Champion

U.S. Army
Third Armored Division, Light Heavyweight

1959-Champion
1960-Champion

Third Armored Division, Track and Field

1960-Third Place, Shot-put

Civilian

1961-KCMO, Light Heavyweight Champion 1961-(summer)-KCMO/St. Louis, State Heavyweight Champion

1962-KCK, Golden Gloves Heavyweight Champion

1962-Wichita, Ks., Golden Gloves Light Heavyweight Champion

1964-Missouri Valley, AAU Heavyweight Champion

1964-Las Vegas, Nevada, and National AAU Tournament: Lost in Quarter Finals (at 189 lbs.) to Buster Mathes (at 293 lbs.) by split decision (Buster Mathes went on to be world heavyweight champion).

Wesley Walker's Boxing Record:

97 wins

11 losses

1 decision

Summer wheelchair Sports

National 1968 Champion Shot Put
National 1968 Champion Discus

Pan American Game Track and Field
Buenos-Aries Argentina 1969
Gold – Silver - Bronze
Shot Put
Discus
Javelin

Pan American Games 1971
Kington Jamaica Track and Field
(3) Three Gold Metals
Shot Put
Discus
Javelin

Letters

The thing I think about most, is Wesley Walker was a quiet, friendly, good human being. He always had a good solid smile that made you feel good.

Wesley was one of the best all-around athletes in the history of Lawrence, Kansas, "Great boxer" and wonderful basketball player.

But again, his humble approach to life is what I respected most.

Thanks,

John Hadl

WESLEY WALKER, MY FRIEND

Many surveys throughout the years have centered upon athletics and the "best" to ever play the "game". The fascination of comparisons through time has generated excitement for all of us, as we look and remember those athletes and sport legends of today and yester-year. The great KU Coach "Phog" Allen, when asked to name his best players, merely stated that he needed to wait 20 years after graduation before the "best" would finally distinguish themselves. From that statement, one would surmise that the "best" or a "top ten listing" might be something more than points scored, yards gained, or medals won. Maybe a combination of flexibility, balance, agility, strength, and endurance molded with desire, integrity, humility, and effort can set the formula or guidelines for athletic achievement. Add to the equation, life lessons in citizenship and morality, hardship and recovery, and giving back to society, as the final chapter in selecting the "best".

As a Lawrence High School graduate ('56), and later an athlete, coach, and Physical Education faculty member at the University of Kansas (retired 2002), I wish to reminisce to the times in the 1950's when a young African American LHS student exhibited sport skills that were, to that point, new and exciting to coaches, fans, and fellow athletes. He was a quiet, reserved young man that simply had "God given" physical talent. He was faster, quicker, and stronger than his peers, and his agility and athletic expertise was soon recognized and recruited by a multitude of sport enthusiasts. It is hard to imagine a young high school kid so far above the curve. He played basketball for various town teams, using ball handling and scoring skills only matched by the Harlem Globe Trotters, and he became a ranking boxer in the light heavy weight division. His basketball accomplishments are remarkable, even at the professional level, and his boxing legacy in Lawrence, Kansas is legendary. He was ambidextrous, equal with both hands, and quick as a cat. He boxed right handed and left handed with power and speed, and his courage in the ring was unmatched. He was a founding father for the Lawrence Boxing Club, and through the years, a coach, trainer, and mentor for countless young boys. Of course, I am speaking from my association, admiration, and from my heart of the "Magical" Wesley Walker. He is a man to this day who can brighten a room just by his presence, and create immense respect even through his silence. He is a "role model" for role models, and one of the finest men and athletes that I have had the privilege to call a "friend".

Early in his adult life Wesley was involved in a single vehicle roll-over accident. It was on a curvy County road north of the city he grew up in. Wesley was pinned under the car, his legs shattered by the trauma. In a blink of an eye, Wesley's destiny was altered. James Naismith, The Inventor of Basketball, once said: "Adversity gives us opportunity". In the case of Wesley Walker, truer words were never spoken. After a lengthy recovery period, Wesley eventually progressed from bed to wheel chair, and later to canes and crutches. His competitive spirit and enthusiasm for life led him even further into the sport arena. He became a boxing coach, he competed in wheelchair basketball, and he became successful in private business. As a coach he was a life-changer for many young boys, and in basketball he became a Wheelchair All American for his prowess and ball handling skills on the court.

After my retirement from KU I built a home north of Lawrence, Kansas, near the very curve that changed Wesley Walker's life. I think of him often, and visit with him occasionally, but I realize now that life experiences should be taken proudly and with gratitude. Wesley's destiny has not been dampened by complaints, anger, or excuses. He is a great example of trust and integrity, courage and energy, and self confidence and respect. Twenty years after he hung up the gloves, and put the basketball in storage, Wesley Walker has more than earned the title of "best". He was an incredible athlete with skills beyond belief. He became a "man among men" who chose "never to have a bad day". I salute you Wesley for your magical brand on sport and athletics, and I will always be grateful for your talent, inspiration, courage, and friendship.

Bob Lockwood, Retired
University of Kansas Faculty and Coach

Larry A Hatfield

3703 Tucker Trail
Lawrence, Kansas
Phone 785 764 2307
lhat@sunflower.com

Mr. Jesse Newman,

It is my pleasure to address, to you, some of my memories of Mr. Wesley Walker.

I first became aware of Wes when I was a youngster hanging around Lawrence Lion football practices and games. My first recall was that of seeing his fantastic quickness. His hand and feet were so remarkably fast. I had not seen anyone stick out above the crowd so much before. In the same time period I then recall two high schools boys about to get in a fight in front of the high school at 14th and Mass. They were doing a lot of taunting and posturing when Wesley walked up his presence seemed to frighten both prospective fighters. Wes finally told them to move on because they were both to afraid to fight. They did not challenge Wes. He calmly broke up the situation. At that time I did not know of his great fighting abilities. At this time in my life many of us were constantly gaining entrance into Robinson Gym and the Robinson Annex. John Hadl and I were frequently together playing basketball in these two places. I remember being amazed at seeing this young guy, Wes, being better, much better, than the Jayhawk players. He could simply dribble around them or shoot over them.

I lost track of Wes for a few years and then he was back in my life for awhile. I was working for Wayne Bly with the Lawrence Recreation Department when he started showing up at the gym. Once again it was readily apparent that he was a very fine man. Very gentle but with a commanding presence. I was able to get Wes to play on our Slowbreaks basketball team. What a difference he made to our team. We already had several excellent athletes, like Hadl and Doyle Schick, but Wes made everyone so much better. He was a team player and an enforcer. During one game against the Sigma Nu Fraternity, mostly KU athletes, including Bob Robben, my roommate from the KU football team. Bob, in a moment of haste, squared off on Wes. I jumped in between the two. Wes just stood there without flinching an inch. Bob kept doing a lot of talking until I convinced him it was in his best interests to calm down. Later, on hearing the reputation of Wes, Bob thanked me. I assured him that I saved him serious damage although Bob had no fear of anyone. At some point in this approximate time span I had always heard that Wesley went off to be the dribbler for Marcus Haynes and his Harlem Magicians. I guarantee you he could perform that role.

At some point, around 1961 or 1962, I recall joining Wesley's boxing club. The Tornadoes I believe. We trained over a car dealership as I recall. Believe it was Parker Buick at around 700 New Hampshire. I knew Wes had won Golden Gloves crowns but he was coaching at this time. Wes felt our team could beat Gateway Sporting Goods for the club championship. Our best boxer, Ron Marsh, quit our team and joined Gateway. That rankled Wesley. At the last minute he decided to enter. Long story short he fights Ron for the title. In one great fight they gave the tie to Ron as he was the defending champion. Ron went on and had a good professional career but Wesley fought him to a draw while past his prime and with very little training.

All in all Wesley Walker is a first class gentleman, one great athlete and has been a good friend. It was always a pleasure to be around him.

Respectfully,

64

Wesley Walker

What I know about Wesley Walker. As I was going up as a kid, I knew him as a basketball player. He would always talk to us kids, over at Pinckney Elementary school and Clinton Park located in West Lawrence. He would always be sitting on his porch watching us kids play sports, basketball, football, and baseball. Most all the kids in the neighborhood knew Wesley Walker. When us kids where about 13 or 14 he would usually join us in a game…most likely basketball…if you where on his team…you would have to be ready for the ball at all times. He played like the Harlem Globetrotters. No look passes, bounce pass, and trick passes, if you weren't ready for it. Most general you would be hit in the nose mouth, and head. Also, you better be hustling at all times, if you played on his team…He would always tell us hurry up, move, move, Go Go Go…

He enjoyed working with kids…especially if you worked hard and like sports…he wanted you to be the best you could be…he knew who were the athletes and who wanted to be the best they could be.

Later as I grew up…remembering him in the Golden Gloves…he wanted me to box…I played competition sports in High School…so I wasn't able to box. I played Basketball, Football, Track, and Baseball.

After graduating from High School I played on his brothers' basketball team Howard Walker. Later on Wesley and I played on a different team together. The Slow Breakers, along with Willis Brooks, Larry Hatfield, John Hadl, Francis Ludvicek, and Tom Boyd. The following year, I played on a different team, Bob Billings, Monte Johnson, Doyle Schick, and John Hadl.

Wesley moved out of town, and I seen him off and on through out the years.

I will always remember Wesley for not letting me buy the bicycle frame under the front porch of his mom and dad's house.

That is what I remember about Wesley Walker growing up in Lawrence, Kansas

In the year of 1997 we had a big family reunion over at Clinton Park on 5th street across the street from his brother Howard Walker's house. That was the last time I seen or talked to Wesley. I have heard he lives in the Old Salsbury house. I guess I will get to see him at the special dinner for Wesley.

Willie Mumford

Willie Mumford

10-13-08

Re: Coach Walker

Wes was a real lover of sports.

He _gave_ much of himself to athletics.

He worked hard coaching and sparing with myself to prep me for the K.C. ~~Golden Gloves~~ during the years of 1962 and 63.

Wes fought me in the 1963 Golden Gloves.

I was very nervous prior to the bout, for he was a better boxer than myself.

To this day I believe that he ~~gave~~ me the bout.

Sincerely,
Ron Marsh

Wesley Walker

Wow, What an athlete and a great guy. I was very courante in my younger years to be under Wesley's watch. He taught me how to play football and basketball on the playgrounds at Pickney School. My dad used to pick me up on his way home every night at 6:00. I was the only white boy on the court or playground and Wesley watched over me for all of my grade school years. I owe him many thanks for all of the advice and support he came to me. He was one of the finest and most gifted athletes I have ever seen or played with or against. He was before his time. His was what I call an "it", very special. Most of all Wesley was a very humble and gracious person. I must say I am very happy to call Wesley my friend, I hope this finds you in good spirits and health.

TB

Tom Black
1960 Avenida La Posta
Encinitas, CA 92024

October 18, 2002

I knew Wesley Walker a little over fifty years ago. I played intra-mural sports with Wes for a few years.

I met him playing basketball at the Lawrence Community Building gym at 11th and Vermont Street, across from Capital Federal. We would choose up sides and play a game. Some of the players were Don Jaimes (one-time Central Junior High School principal); Larry Campbell (one-time principal at Vinland School);Buster Carney (coach and teacher at South Junior High); Bob Lockwood (gym coach at KU); and many LHS students and athletes.

Wes was by far the best. He would out-shoot, out-dribble, out-pass, out-fake anyone out there. He definitely knew the game of basketball. Once in a while, I would have to guard him. He would go through all kinds of fake motions and dribble by me leaving me dumb-founded. All in all it did make me a better ballplayer.-never like him though-he was amazing. He did these feats humbly, no trash talk, very sportsman-like.

Wes also played touch football with us at the KU fields, across from what is now the *Dole Center*. LHS students, alums, and ex-LHS football players. Don't remember his football feats as much as his basketball, but do remember he was very good.

Wes was good at any sport he approached: basketball, football, boxing, wrestling. (don't know about baseball). Wes is not a tall man, but very strong physically. He will try to beat you fair and square. Wes is a tribute to all Lawrence sport competiveness and sportsmanship. He made me a better player and person.

Bob Altenbend

I have Known Wesley Walker for about 55yrs. I first met Wesley while In Junior high + High School. I was going from Junior high to High School In the afternoon to my F.F.A. farm class. I was Confronted one afternoon after School by 2 Brothers both older + Bigger than me. Things looked Bad then Wes Came along Some words were exchaned + they took off. I was very Gratful to Wes for Stoping In. Thats just the way Wes was. He was friendly, had a way with words, but had a lot of Authority about him. Wes was Respectful + everyone I met Respected him. Wesley had a 1947 Chev that the Brakes were Completely Gone. I was In Auto mechanics Class so I took Wesleys Car In + fixed It. He was very Gratful. It was the Start of an everlasting friendship. As the years progessed our friendship further developed through our Maturity + Respect for each other. Wesley + myself were on the first Boxing team or Club to Repesent Lawrence In 1954. It was Coached by John Lawrence + Marvin Lipp. We Competed at the Topeka Kansas Golden Gloves tournment Just before Wes + I left for Service. Wes had Great Suxess with his Basketball Expertise. He was a member of the Harlem Jesters, a profesional basket Ball Team + toured + played all around. While In Service In Germany Wes had great Suxess with Boxing, Basketball, + track winning many medals. I went to Korea

Wes & I lost Contact until we returned from Service. I had a Tree Business & Wes went to work for me. He was the best worker I ever had We took out 385 Big Elm trees that year 1961. Wes decided to train for the Golden Gloves Championship In Kansas City mo In 1961. He won the Championship Successfuly. Wes was preparing for a Repeat the next year. But Beset with bad weather cond. & distance made traveling to K.C. very diffucult. Wes & I had a Idea to try & Start a club Here In Lawrence. We were exicited & Started putting It together. With the help of Wesely's father "Glen" & Brother Howard we found an old pool Hall at 735 ½ New Hampshire and proceeded to turn It Into a real nice Boxing club. & gym It was Great Wes could train at home. & the club grew quickley with new members. Wes lived In an appartment across the Hall. The club Grew & turned out some good athletes. Wes had a very bad Car accident that mangaled his leg. He worked through the pain while In a cast He was amazing. He had a real bad Itch down Inside the cast. & took a coat Hanger cut It. He could stick It down Inside the cast & Scratch It. At that point he said that felt better than a climax. I was there for Wes through this ordeal. When Wes moved to Chicago I really missed him. I moved to Calif. with my family to be there for

71

my sister who had a heart attack. In this time Wes & I were busy getting settled & restarted In different cities we moved talls and never lost our feelings & friendship. I came back from Calif for good when my father died In 1974. I went to Chicago One time to see Wes It was great to see him but I didn't like the City. Wes's father died & then His mother died. Wes came back for these Sad times, also to Check on properties that he had. We always got together & I tried to take care of Some of the problems with them. When I got a case & had to do some time In 1985 Wes came back to be here for me. He took this time off just for me, His apperance & presence were really felt by everyone, Especially the judge & prosecter, He even came back & saw me In prison. Wesley Walker Is my brother. Im here & here for him & he Is for me. Through the years & the presence, Wes has been fighting to save his leg. He Is a true Christian man & has more faith & strength than any man I've ever met. He Is working with this Ordeal keeping his faith & being strong

In regards to Wesley B. Walker my trusted friend I would like to Conclude with Quote "He Is But One" But he Is one, he Cannot do everything, But he can do Something, & that what he can do he Should do, & by the grace he will do.
(of God)
Gary Lee Thomas

LES STECKEL

27 NOV 2008
(Thanksgiving)

Wesley,

Please accept my sincere appreciation for your major contribution to my life. Your professional & personal training in the Golden Gloves has given me a life-long confidence & self-assurance that allowed me to reach several achievements in life that many will never experience.

I am truly grateful for you and your Dad for "talking me into" boxing for you & your team you assembled. It was an honor & a great pleasure to re-connect with you. God speed! Les Steckel

Wesley Walker is a true Lawrence hero.
Many people will remember that he saved a well known
local disabled man by interrupting a late night robbery in
an alley in downtown Lawrence, where the tiny man was
sleeping in his homemade cart. He chased the robber, caught
him, & held him for the police.

He coached the Lawrence boxing team & took them
to Kansas City to appear in Golden Gloves tournaments. Once we
went together and as he introduced me to coaches & people running
the events I saw how many people knew & how they liked &
respected him as a coach & as a boxer.

By the life he led he set an example for others.
People in Lawrence noticed the good work he was doing with
teenagers. Jack Mitchell was the K.U. football coach
at that time. He offered the use of KU's athletic
facilities in the training room for the boxers with bumps &
bruises. Wesley was very proud of that.

Once on the spur of the moment he was talked
into entering the Golden Gloves in Los Vegas, where he fought
Buster Mathis who won, & later fought professionally as a
heavyweight. As he was telling me about it he said,
with a twinkle in his eye: "you know I could have won that
fight if I had trained for it."

Things don't always go well for heroes. When he was on the verge of starting a new job in Lawrence that would make full use of his talents, he was in a terrible auto accident that left one leg damaged for life.

Many months later this soft spoken, deep voiced man quietly went north to a college community where took a job in charge of lab facilities. He never complained.

I remember receiving a post card from him some time later. You could not keep him down. He was in South America + had just won a gold medal throwing the discus in the International Wheelchair Olympics, + was already planning a trip to another meet — I think it was in Spain or Europe somewhere.

Over the years we would talk on the telephone + when he was in town he would sometimes stop by my office just to visit. He could deal with frustrating problems in his life and keep on going with an inner strength not many people have. That is what heroes do.

Count me among his admirers.

RALPH M. KING, JR.

Rev. Deacon Dr. Jesse Milan, Ed. D
7103 Waverly Avenue
Kansas City, Kansas 66109

Phone: (913) 334 – 0366   Fax: (913) 334 – 2032   e-mail: jmilan@myexcel.com-

October 17, 2008

Mr. Jesse Newman
415 Illinois Street
Lawrence, Kansas 6604

Dear Jesse,

Enclosed is my statement about Wesley Walker. Thanks for the opportunituy to

submit this brief contriution abour a vry fine person. Good luck on your

endeavor to record a positive record about a youth of Lawrence.

Sincerely,

Jesse Milan

WESLEY WALKER

I am pleased to submit this statement on behalf of my friend Wesley Walker. I have known him for over 39 years. During the time of our close association was while he was a student in the Lawrence Public Schools. He was an individual who experienced many hardships as an African American in Lawrence. For during those days there was much discrimination because of race. African Americans were denied equal housing, public accommodations, employment opportunities. Further, extra curricular activities. Wesley was told by the basketball coach that he was too good to make the team. That didn't cause Wesley to deviate from his basic being. For Wesley was the type of student, and person to take adversity and turn it into something positive. Such gave him the strength to face adversity and positive attitude and pursuit in life.

During those days, I was Director of the Pinckey Playground. Wesley was a silent leader among other youth of his age and younger. He had, and did have, the last time I saw him, that positive attitude. He was what I called a silent leader. He did not boost or force his way or will on others, He would join a gathering and in his silent way, cause the gathering to move in positive actions. If a game was not going well, He, Wesley would render his efforts to encourage "team" work in playing the game or solving the problem that resulted in poor action or performance. He always strived to be the best he could be and do the best he could for the betterment of the gathering or group.

It was a pleasure to have such a participant on my Playground. Also, as a friend in the community. Our paths crossed not just on Pinckney Playground, but through the community of Lawrence. He was always respectful, positive and willing to do what he could to make life better for others and himself. Wesley was not a selfish person. He was a joy to work with and to have as a friend. I could go on for several more pages, but I will bring my comments to closure with this statement.

Wesley, was a talented individual and used his knowledge and skills to make whatever situation he found himself, better for those around him, and in the end for himself.

I was blessed to have had him as a supporter and friend during those dark days of discrimination in Lawrence back in the 50' and 60'.

Newspaper Clippings/Articles

GOOSE HAS LAST LAUGH—Goose Tatum, often referred to as the "Clown Prince of Basketball" will perform at 8:30 o'clock Thursday night against the Kentucky Colonels in the Municipal Auditorium.

Haskell Warriors Capture League Crown; Braves and Puds Close

The Haskell Warriors swung past the All Stars Monday night to take the City League Tournament championship. This is their first crown this year, as they were last in the city league playoffs.

The championship was won last year by the FFA, but the boys didn't have the stuff this year to stay in the fight.

The two other Haskell teams took second and third places, thus giving Haskell complete domination in the tournament.

In the final games of the tournament, the Grey Eagles fell to the Braves after building up a nine point lead early in the game. The Braves were red hot in the second half and came out shooting. They took the lead at 3rd period and barely managed to hold it, as they went on to win 34-33.

At LMHS, the Little Lions nosed out the FFA in an overtime 42-38 after fouling out the FFA big

guns, Tate and Cawley. The Little Lions were sparked by Danny Jaimes who collected 14, and the FFA was kept in the game by Cawley, who hit for 20 before fouling out.

The Cubs shot past the Puds, handing them a 47-30 thrashing. The young Lions were at their peak for this game, and Emory and Lester Smith racked point after point on smooth working fast breaks.

Scoring honors for the evening went to Wesley Walker, who hit 18 points, and was the Puds main pain under the back boards.

SEASON RECORD
CITY LEAGUE TEAMS

All Stars	9	1	.900
Cubs	9	1	.900
Braves	9	1	.900
FFA	3	7	.300
Grey Eagles	3	7	.300
Puds	3	7	.300
Warriors	6	4	.400

---

at in the city league the L.M.H.S. teams ays tough and hust- as the Haskell All les around the Grey the Braves sweated over the Little Lions. rs had little trouble e cold but hustling by a score of 28-56. it the damper on the 3-21.

the Cubs met and Warriors to the tune the Puds won their the season 47-38 over

arrior game, Wesley rub, poured in 14 the scoring honors while Anderson of put in 9 to lead his

surprise of the eve- hen the last place the FFA. The Puds, Jack Metz and Don red 19 and 13 points ad little trouble af- t quarter.

andings In Boy's ty League

	5	0	1.000
	4	1	.800
	5	1	.833
	3	3	.500
	2	3	.400
	2	3	.333
	1	4	.250
s	1	5	.200

FRIDAY, MARCH 21, 1952

Grid Letter Awards To 25 Lion Players

Twenty-five boys on the 1953 Lawrence High School football team that tied for the Northeast Kansas League title and wound up among the top five teams in the state for the third straight year have been awarded letters.

Included on the list are 12 seniors, 11 juniors and two sophomores. Coach Allan Woolard points out that the heaviest losses this year will be at the tackle and end spots —particularly at tackle. Two managerial letters were also awarded.

Boys receiving letters for 1953 are:

Freddie Cole, junior guard; Charlie Coleman, junior halfback; Gary Creamer, junior quarterback; Jerry Cunningham, sophomore quarterback; Bob Endacott, senior tackle; Max Malott, junior halfback; Terry Malott, senior fullback; Eddie Martin, senior end; Newton McCluggage, senior end; Gene Mullin, senior tackle; Tommy Parker, junior guard; John Pierson, senior tackle; Fred Ramirez, senior halfback; Jim Rose, junior center; Richard Skinner, junior quarterback; Lester Smith, senior halfback; William Smith, sophomore halfback; Bob Stauffer, senior halfback; Bruce Tate, junior end; Jaydee Stinson, junior guard; Mike Thomas, senior halfback; Leslie Walker, senior end; John Wertzberger, senior tackle; Pete Whitright, junior fullback; Max Williams, junior guard.

GUY BARNES, LMHS head track coach begins his second season as mentor of the thinclads. His first season last year was one of the best in recent annals of the cinder sport at Lawrence. Placing second in the NEK League meet and fifth in the State competition, the squad rolled up a commendable record. With eleven returning lettermen he ____ better season

30, 1953

First Team of All-Stars Dominated By Seniors; Cawley and Easum Stars

This year in selecting an LMHS city league all-star basketball team each of the five coaches representing the LMHS city-league teams were asked to pick an all-opponent team. Each was also asked to pick his team's most valuable player.

Each all-opponent selection was counted as one point and each valuable player received one-half point. From the voting Darrel Easum and Bob Cawley were the only unanimous selections after all votes were counted.

Starting at forward positions on the first team are Darrel Esum, Gray Eagles, and Wesley Walker of the Cubs. Although these two boys are not giants, no team was quite able to stop the terrific scoring pace they set throughout the season. Walker counted for many of his baskets by his unusual ability to break behind the defense for a lay-in shot. Easum will long be remembered for the fabulous sum of 33 points he accounted for in one game. He was always capable of making it rough for his opponents.

Playing at the center or post position is Don Rake. Don was a B Squad letterman last year and gained valuable experience there. Don was an aggressive rebounder and he did a good share of the scoring for the Puds.

Rounding out the starting line-up Jack Metz and Bob Cawley were placed at the guard positions. Both boys were strong scoring threats as they could hit from any position on the court. Cowley, the taller of the two, was a great rebounder and floor player. Metz also snared quite a few rebounds and was noted for his almost unguardable jump shot.

considered him as the most improved player in the City League.

Marquette and Jaimes together carried much of the burden of their teams' scoring. Marquette in many games took top scoring honors with Jaimes close behind. Other teams represented on the second five were the FFA and the Gray Eagles by Lanny Tate and Frank Willingham respectively. Lanny although hampered with illness his last few games, was always a standout for the FFA. Teaming up with Bob Cawley he added punch to the FFA scoring attack. Frank Willingham another one of last year's B squad lettermen, was a big help to the Grey Eagles. He was a good rebounder, consistant scorer and a fine ball handler.

Other boys who received points besides those who were able to land a berth on either the first or second all-star team were: Ken Elliot, Gray Eagles, Leo Williams, Puds, and Fred Pickens, Little Lions.

The Haskell players due to an insufficient amount of information were not included in the selecti___

First Team
F	Walker—Cubs
F	Easum—Grey Eagles
C	Rake—Puds
G	Metz—Puds
G	Cawley—FFA

Second Team
F	Marquette—Little Lions
F	Willingham—Grey Eagles
C	Estes—Little Lions
G	Jaimes—Little Lions
G	Tate—FFA

Friday, Octo

Gym Reco

A jump of 10" LMHS standing br ord for the boys Thursday, October was Thomas Ragl member of the Tu fourth hour gym cl The record-break place while the participating in th ng carried on to o ral ability.

Boys' Cage Teams Start Regular Season

The boy's city cage loop opened regular season play Monday, with eight quintets clashing in the limelight. In the lid opener on LMHS planks, Senior 2 smashed the F. F. A., 64-50, with Don Beene, who dumped in 16 points, and Fred Pickens, who cut the cords with 14 counters, leading the bucket brigade. Merle Schneck led the losers with 17 points. The game was highlighted by the 37 point scoring spree by the F. F. A. in the last half; however, the Seniors could afford it as they had already stashed away enough points to win the tilt.

In the second skirmish, the Little Lions demolished the hapless Cubs, 59-23. Wes Walker did most of the damage by chalking up 20 points. The win-hungry Cubs tried to stop Walker and the Little Lions, but their trial was in vain.

In the Haskell teepee, the All-Stars thrashed Senior 1, but by all means they didn't do it easily. The Seniors came out in the third quarter to cut the big Injun half-time margin to three points. And allergic to the Haskell floor as they are, Senior team 1 fell to their powerful foes, 43-38. Other teams in the city hoop loop had better not take the upset minded Senior 1 team too lightly, because as their five point loss to the city tournament victors indicate, they can dish out plenty of trouble.

In the other cage powwow, the Warriors scalped the Braves in a thriller to notch their first league win.

Last week, the All-Stars captured first place in the pre-season tournament with an impressive 49-41 win over Senior 2. The hoopsters from Haskell had a well-balanced attack in their last quarter bucket bombardment. However, high point man in the conflict was LeRoy Logan who netted 14 counters, swishing six field goals and two via the charity toss.

The unpredictable Cubs fought F. F. A. down to the wire and finally unleashed a 29-26 verdict over their foes. This dropped the F. F. A. at the bottom of the tournament barrel and gave the Cubs undisputed seventh place.

Next Monday, the second round will be played with the eight teams again colliding.

It looks as if the league will be centered around the All-Stars, Little Lions, and Senior 2, and from the way it looks, that's the way they'll probably finish.

A couple of stars have struck out in the City League play. For the boys, Wesley Walker has been a common favorite in the first games of the young season, scoring 20 points in the Little Lion's game with the Cubs. A regular Marcus Haines, Wes is headed for All-Star. For the feminine basketeers, Joanie Underwood has been the big gun, displaying easy, natural co-ordination and grace under the cords. Other high scorers for the Girl's City League are Betty Carter, of the Bunnyhoppers; Marilyn Perry, Little Lionesses; and Katy Dunnigan of the Speedy Six.

All-Stars Leading League; Cellar Dwellers Victorious

Only one team was left unbeaten as the result of Monday's City cage games. This quintet was the All-Stars who held the undefeated perch by conquering the Little Lions 56-55 on LMHS timber. The Haskellites were helped by their blood brothers, the Braves, who subdued Senior II, previously untamed in league play.

The All-Stars exchanged buckets with the Little Lions shortly after the tipoff but that's as close as it got during the first quarter. With the LMHS lads trailing 16-6, Wes Walker, the playmaker of the Lion pack, came into the court riot. With his quick reflexed and beautiful ball handling, Walker and company was able to whittle down the bulky lead to a mere few points. The game wasn't the only thing that went wild as the crowd was also in the mood of the thrilling affair. Walker was pronounced guilty of his fifth and last personal foul late in the last quarter but the Little Lion hustle still went on. The game horn sounded and the All-Stars had crushed the Little Leos by one point to put them on top of the hoop heap, the spot in which they will probably keep throughout conference play. Walker garnered high scoring laurels with 24 points. The All-Stars also beat the Little Lions in the opening round of the pre-season tournament, ousting them 44-42.

In the preliminary, the Cubs upset Senior I 47-43, to give the puzzled seniors undisputed possession of the cellar, something which they will be glad to pass on to some other team. The Cubs were hotter than a Bunsen burner, hitting 52 per cent of their field goal attempts while Senior I was just luke warm. The seniors trailed throughout the contest but that didn't slow down their attack. Earl Church was the center of activity as the plays were built around him. Church was high point man of the conflict by netting 26

counters, mainly with the use of his unstoppable left hook. He was also plagued at the free throw line as he missed 12 attempts, although many of his points were made at the black stripe. Max Williams, the sophomore basketball machine, paced his team mates by dumping 14 points through the rim.

Lawrence, Kansas, Wednesday

Here is the rost who are now liste the Lawrence Hig football squad. A ing the name den The squad:

EN
Name
Don Elliott
Dale Flory
Dick Laing
*Newt McClugga
*Ed Martin
Bruce Tate
Wes Walker
Bob Walters
TAC
Dean Elliott
*Bob Endacott
*Gene Mullin
*John Pierson
Alan Robb
Bob Rogers
*John Wertzberger
GUA
Bud Cole
*Tom Parker
Bill Stead
Jaydee Stinson
Ron Tisue
Max Williams
CEN
Bob Allison
Jim Rose
Phil Stuart
QUARTE
*Gary Creamer
Jerry Cunningham
Richard Skinner
*Lester Smith
HALF
Charles Coleman
Joe Eichhorn
Ronald Johnson
*Joe Malott
Gary Odaffer
Burton Pontius
*Fred Ramirez
William Smith
Bob Stauffer
*Mike Thomas
FULL
Don Acher
*Terry Malott
Pete Whitenight

CAN IT BE?

Who at Beeline holds a World Record in athletic competition? Who at Beeline recently competed in a big Pan American athletic meet in Buenos Aires? Who at Beeline holds a national discus record? At this point you may think we're joking, but the fact is that such a gentleman works here every day, quietly performing his duties in the Shipping Department.

Meet Wes Walker, our Padlocker Operator. Before leaving for Buenos Aires in February, Wes already held U. S. records in the shot put and discus throw, but at the Pan American Wheelchair Games, Wes set his world record of exactly 33 feet.

Wes setting new World Record for wheelchair shot put.

Prior to an auto accident in which he suffered permanent injury to his legs, Wes was a serious amateur boxer and boxing coach, as well as a promising football player. Among his boxing accomplishments during the period from 1955 to 1964 were the light-heavyweight titles in the Topeka Kansas Golden Gloves; Kansas City, Kansas Golden Gloves; 3rd Armored Division title; Kansas City, Missouri Golden Gloves; Springfield, Missouri Golden Gloves; Wichita, Kansas Golden Gloves; and Missouri Valley AAU title. Of his 97 fights, he won 86, of which 14 were by decision and 72 by knock-out. He was awarded an athletic scholarship to Idaho State University, but was forced to relinquish it after being injured in football.

At one time Wes was the lead scorer (avg. 30 points a game) for the Harlem Jesters, the farm team for the world famous Harlem Globetrotters basketball team.

Two years after his accident, Wes moved from Kansas to Downers Grove, where he was first exposed to the Chicago Sidewinders Wheelchair sports club. The Chicago Sidewinders compete in basketball, swimming, archery, table tennis, weightlifting and other events both nationally and internationally. After just two years with the Sidewinders, Wes was chosen to represent the U.S.A. in the Pan American Wheelchair sports competition.

The team spent most of their 3 week stay in Buenos Aires where the games were held this February. The last week was spent in Rio de Janeiro.

Wes receiving 2nd team All-Tourney Basketball Award.

Seven Local Boxers Working for Gloves

Seven local boxers currently are drilling under handlers Marvin Lipp and John Lawrence for the regional Golden Gloves tournament Jan. 26-27-28 at Topeka's Municipal Auditorium.

Lipp and Lawrence this week issued the call for all interested in competing in the Capital City event. The group is working out daily at 421 Pleasant St. There is room on the squad for more battlers. Lipp may be phoned after 5 p. m. at 1379-M or may be contacted in person.

Presently on the team are: Heavyweight Owen Jones, 20 years old and 195 pounds of 1420 R. I. St.; light heavyweights Tony Setter, 19, 165, 1126 O. St., and Wesley Walker, 18, 170, 512 Ill. St.; middleweight Frank Toney, 20, 149, 211 Tenn. St.; welterweight Myron Feuborn, 19, 145, 1126 O. St.; featherweight Andy Johnson, 18, 125, 211 Tenn. St.; paperweight Bobby Nitsch, 11, 75, 1005 N. H. St.

Lipp and Lawrence agree their crew has shown extreme willingness to work and improve in drills to date and view the chances for the Topeka meet optimistically.

"Desire is actually about 99 per cent of boxing, and our boys certainly have that," Lipp says. "John and I figure we'll do okay in the Gloves."

January 26, 1954.

Lawrence Golden Glovers To Go to Topeka Tonight For Exams, Draws, Bouts

The Lawrence contingent for the Golden Gloves will go to Topeka tonight for physical examinations and drawings for opponents. Some of the boys will compete tonight.

The event will run tonight, Wednesday and Thursday nights.

Coach Marvin Lipp and assistant Bill Hunsinger will be accompanied tonight by:

Sonny Peters, 157, middleweight; Gary Thomas, 160, middleweight; Willie Smith, 155, middleweight; Wesley Walker, 175, light heavyweight; Fred Atchison, 135, lightweight; Larry Smith, 125, featherweight; Thomas Ragland, 147, welterweight; Vernon Smith, 160, middleweight; Dalton Vann, 95, paperweight.

Heavyweight Ward Jones, 190, will be unable to go tonight since he must work as an officer on the Lawrence Police Department. Jones will compete Wednesday night.

The open class competition will consist of three two-minute rounds while the novice class competition will consist of three 90-second rounds.

The Lawrence boxers will not know whom they will fight until the drawings tonight.

LAWRENCIAN ENROUTE TO VICTORY—Wes Walker (right), Lawrence 175-pounder, has Marvin Holmes, Ottawa, in trouble in this scene from Walker's Tuesday night decision over the 1954 Ottawa High's football fullback in the Topeka Golden Gloves tourney. Walker will meet Rusty Schwerdt of Topeka for the light heavyweight title Friday night.

Lawrence Glovers Invade Topeka

Displaying a lethal one-two punch—revolver in his right hand, fist-filled boxing glove in his left—is Lawrence policeman Ward Jones, the standout member of the Lawrence team that will begin competition in the Topeka Golden Gloves tonight. Jones, a 195-pounder with over 100 amateur fights, will compete in the open class and is a strong favorite. Jones and the rest of the city team handled by

Marvin Lipp (left) and John Lawrence (right) have been working out steadily for the Capital City affair. Left to right in this shot are Lipp, Wes Walker, Jones, Elmer Robinson, Bobby Nitsch, little fellow by Jones, who'll compete as a paperweight, Tom Ragland, Emery Hamm, Charles Newman and Lawrence Jones, by the way, has been out of the ring about five years. The last time he fought he weighed 140. (Journal-World Photo).

Senior B Court Champion

Senior B of Lawrence High annexed the Boys' City League basketball title last week with a 45 to 41 win over the Braves of Haskell. Allison led the Senior B attack with 14 points. Wesley (Goose) Walker played an outstanding floor game for the winners. In other games, the Warriors walloped the Frosh 67 to 54. Little Lions 55 FFA 38; Senior A 59 Cubs 31. The teams started a tournament Monday.

Standings

Team	Won	Lost
Senior B	7	0
Braves	5	2
Warriors	5	2
Senior A	4	3
Little Lions	3	4
Cubs	2	5
F. F. A.	2	5
Frosh	0	7

'54 Grid Prospect Appears Bright; Backfield Strong

The Lawrence Lions will open their 1954 Football season September 17th against Manhattan in Lawrence. The Lions will boast 14 returning lettermen, including 12 Juniors and 2 Sophomores.

On August 28, the Leos will check out equipment, and on August 30th they will start regular practices.

The Lions will play a nine game schedule, including five games at home. As usual, all home games will be played at Haskell Stadium.

Coaching methods will be the same as this year except for the way the blocking assignments are given. Coach Woolard said that this would be much more simple than the previous method.

Of course all positions will be open, but the positions that will be hardest to get are the tackles and end spots that are left vacant by the graduation of Bob Endacott, Newt McCluggage, Eddie Martin, John Wertzberger and Wes Walker. At the moment the Leos seem to be the deepest in backfield prospects.

Head Coach Woolard stated that there is a promising crop of sophomores coming up from Junior High School. With the usual hard work and hustle the Lions should have another great season in the making.

1954 Schedule

Sept. 17	Manhattan	Here
Sept. 24	Topeka	There
Oct. 1	Atchison	Here
Oct. 8	Shawnee-Mission	Here
Oct. 15	Leavenworth	There
Oct. 22	Argentine	Here
Oct. 29	Ottawa	There
Nov. 5	Wyandotte	There
Nov. 12	Highland Park	Here

Ten Topekans Spice Gloves Card Tonight

With the weather forecast for "fair," Topeka's 16th annual Golden Gloves finals will be fought tonight at Municipal Auditorium with the largest number of local youths in the tournament's history competing for titles.

Ten Topeka boxers will be bidding for Golden Gloves thrones when the gong sends the first fighters together at 8:30.

In the open class heavyweight division, Charles Rome, 215-pound Topekan with a knockout punch, will have at least a 20-pound weight advantage when the pride of Coleman's Athletic Club collides with Joe LaQuarta, muscular Italian from Pittsburgh, Pa., representing Ft. Riley.

Dale Sudduth, clever boxing light heavyweight and brother of professional fighter Billy Sudduth, faces one of Ft. Riley's best in Floyd Washington for the open 175-pound crown.

Topeka, with its best group of novices in recent years, will send I. C. Sanders, 112-pounder, against Charles York of the Boys Industrial School. Edward Harris, Topeka, bids for 118-pound honors, meeting Ray Raymos of the BIS. Freddy Davis, Topeka, throws punches for the 126-pound title, meeting William Reed of BIS.

Two of coach Billy Sudduth's better pupils, Newt Harris and Theodore Wright, meet for the 135-pound lightweight title. Two 147-pound Topeka youths slug it out for the welterweight title when Torrence Cushinberry and Alvin Brodis meet.

Rusty Schwerdt, Topeka knockout ace, fights for the 175-pound light-heavyweight title with Wes Walker of Lawrence.

Tommy Ragland faces Sonny Peters of Lawrence in the 160-pound title bout in the novice ranks. Two of Forbes' bitter heavyweight rivals meet for the novice title when Ed Loskot faces Arthur Little.

Cpl. Rick Echavez, 110-pound open class ace from Hawaii on the Ft. Riley team, faces a tough foe in Don Reynolds of Leavenworth, for the title.

Golden Gloves officials announced should nature play tricks upon the weather man, the fights will go on regardless. Tournament winners will begin fighting Tuesday in the Kansas City tourney.

Fritzel, Comets in Lead For City Hoopster Chase

Fritzel 66 leads the "A" section and the Comets hold top spot in the "B" circuit as play in the City Basketball Leagues nears the halfway mark.

Fritzel edged Douglas County State Bank last week to gain the top spot while the Comets won a close one from Bridge Standard Service. The Fritzel team is composed of former Lawrence High players. It includes Frank Black and Bob Preston, K. U. gridders. The Comets, a Negro team, are led by Wesley Walker, one of the outstanding league players who did not play high school basketball.

Standings:

A-League	Won	Lost
Fritzel 66	4	0
Douglas Co. Bank	3	1
Winter Chevrolet	2	2
Haskell	2	2
Woody Aces	1	3
DeSoto	0	3

B-League	Won	Lost
Comets	5	0
Bridge Standard	4	1
American Legion	3	2
Old-Timers	2	3
Lawrence Paper	1	3
Cyclones	1	4

Dragons Lead City Loop With Wolverines Second

The Dragons edged the Wolverines 65 to 62 Wednesday night to retain top spot in the City League. The Wolverines won over Fritzel Thursday 54 to 50 to remain in second place. The final games of the schedule will be played next week with the feature game on Wednesday at 7:30 p. m. when Haskell and the Dragons clash. Wesley Walker of the Wolverines has taken the scoring lead with 199 points. Everett Brewer of Haskell is in second place with 115.

Standings

	W	L
Dragons		
Wolverines		
Haskell		
Fritzel		
Bridge Standard		
Park Hill		

LAST WEEK'S RESULTS

Dragons 65, Wolverines 62; Park Hill 63, Bridge Standard 41; Haskell 49, Bridge Standard 39; Wolverines 54, Fritzel 50.

NEXT WEEK'S SCHEDULE

Feb. 15 — 7:30 Dragons vs. Haskell; 8:30 Park Hill vs. Walkers.
Feb. 16 — Dragons vs. Bridge Standard.

Dragons Win City Loop With Win Over Standard

The Dragons split two games during the week and walked off with the City Adult Basketball League Title. They were defeated by Haskell 61 to 51 and downed Standard 56 to 40 in clincher.

The Wolverines swamped Park Hill Standard 63 to 34 to garner the runner up spot.

Manager of the Dragon team is George Stuart. His players at Robert Cawley, Bill Ward, Lawrence Baber, Jay Williams, Nolan

Braves Edg In Semi-Fin

In the City League semi-finals Monday night ranked Senior B's fell Braves, 39 to 41, while A's were going down to the Cubs eaked out a cl over the Frosh and th won over the Little L 54.

In the opener at the the warriors took an ea hung on to win. Jim A the big gun for the Lit

In the second game, favored Senior A's lost t for the City League championship. The FF still playing their u brand of ball, finally range. This victory against the Braves for pionship next Monday.

At Haskell the Cubs youngsters of the out on even terms right final seconds. Johnny put in 10 counters, potte winning goal for the C seconds to go.

The biggest upset of game in the second g Haskell gym. Perha were over confident. h reporter puts a big qu on the presence of Jol Haskell varsity star, o line up. The B's had night in hitting one o totals. Wes Walker with 17 points lowed with 10 point

Haskell Takes Fi B's Reign in Con

In the City League finals played in the Monda night the Bra championship by edgin 32 to 31. For the fou year the FFA ran into rough and tumble sch more resembled footbal ketbal.

The Braves got off start and led almost with the exception of minute in the fourth qu the FFA pulled up even three point advantage soon erased by the austh Mike Thomas and Bruc the FFA hooped alive the final second.

In the consolation gam ion B's who were exp the tourney ran over th A's 72 to 41. The two even terms through the f ter with the A's scor However, the B's found in the second and open point bulge at the half Both teams substituted o and the reserves really some good performances in the case of the in their rough battle with Gaylord Dav Walker doing the job. ally the B's coming almost all of the

wrence Golden Gloves Hopefuls

Here is the Lawrence group working out each night at the V.F.V Clubrooms for competition in the Topeka Golden Glove Feb. 1, 2 and 4. Marvin Lipp, former Navy ring champ who now perates a beauty salon here, is coach for the group and singer is his assistant. Left to right in this picture are: Assistant oach Hunsinger; Ward Jones, 190, he yyweight; Sonn ight; Gary Thomas, 160, middleweight; Willie Smi 155, middleweight; Wesley Walk light heavywei weight; Larry Smith, 125, feath ight; Tho s Ragland, 147, welterweight; 160, midd coach Lipp (Jo; orld P'

87

...h, Kas.
135-pound class—Terry Lloyd, Sumner
A. C. outpointed Raymond Hand, Leaven-
worth, Kas.
147-pound class—Wordell Banks, Sumner
A. C. scored a first round knockout in
1:01 over Eldridge Davis, Leavenworth,
Kas.
160-pound class—Vernon Smith, Ottawa,
Kas., scored a second round T. K. O. over
Rufus St. Clair, Sumner A. C.
175-pound class—Wesley Walker, Ottawa,
Kas., outpointed Lavelle Stephenson,
Argentine parish house.
Heavyweight class—Don Connelly, Argen-
tine parish house, scored a T. K. O. in
forty-eight seconds of the third round over
Quentin Lamb, Sumner A. C.

Saturday, Feb. 4 . . . 1956

Boys Club Boxers To Golden Gloves

Two Ottawa Boys Club fighters,
Wes Walker and Vernon Smith,
won bouts Saturday night in the
finals of the Golden Gloves preliminaries in Kansas City, Kas.
Smith knocked out his ring foe.
Walker gained a decision.

Both boxers will take part in the
Golden Gloves Tournament of
Champions which opens in the Kansas City, Mo., Municipal Auditorium on Wednesday.

Monday, Feb. 6 1956

Lawrence Boxers Win

Two Lawrence boxers, fighting
under the Ottawa Boys Club ban-
ner, won Golden Gloves preliminary bouts at Kansas City, Kas.,
last night.

Both will be in the preliminary
finals this evening.

Wes Walker, a 175-pounder, gained a split decision over his ring
foe. Vernon "Bunny" Smith,
weighing in at 160, won by a knockout over his opponent in the second round.

If Walker and Smith can come
up with triumphs tonight, they ad-
vance to the Golden Gloves Tournament of Champions which opens
Wednesday in the Kansas City,
Mo., Municipal Auditorium.

3, 1955

Local Boxers Win Four Against Ottawa Youths

Lawrence boxers won four
matches, drew one and lost two
against performers from the Ottawa Boys Club Monday night at
Ottawa.

Three Local Boxers Get Gloves Crowns

Three of the four Lawrence entries in the Kansas City, Kas., Golden Gloves tournament emerged as
champions this week. And the only
raeson the fourth didn't—he was
involved in the finals with a teammate.

The tourney, held this week, was
a Regional meet, and the winners
now go to the Kansas City, Mo.,
Tournament of Champions Feb. 13,
14 and 16 in the Municipal Auditorium.

The Lawrence winners: Novice
light heavyweight, Herky Davenport of Lawrence decisioned Lawrence Redick of Lawrence; novice
heavyweight, Bill Burnison of Lawrence knocked out Richard Scott
of Kansas City in 43 seconds of the
first round with a "powerhouse
right"; and Wesley Walker of Lawrence, fighting in the light heavyweight open division, knocked out
Preston Thomas of Kansas City in
1:43 of the third round. Thomas was
floored in the first round, then
came back in the second to deck
Walker.

Burnison is a Kansas University
freshman football center. On the
basis of this past fall's performance, he is rated as one of the top
prospects off that frosh crew.

Davenport and Burnison both
fought in the novice class.

Lions Rate Edge In NEKL Clash On Tribe Field

Friday Night Contest To Be Shown on TV; Injuries Big Factors

By CLARKE KEYS

A young but furious Northeast Kansas League football rivalry will have its 13th renewal Friday night when the Lawrence Lions and the Shawnee-Mission Indians tangle in Kansas City.

The contest will be the first NEKL game in history to be televised. Station KCTY (25) in Kansas City will air the game. Kickoff time is 8 p. m.

Two Choices for Title

Once again the tilt will match the two favorites for the league title and once again the Leos of Lawrence will rule as slight favorites to hurdle their toughest obstacle in the road to a third straight NEKL crown and the 11th in the last 12 years.

Injuries may play a big part in the game. The Lions will go into the fray with their backfield in sorry shape. Terry Malott, senior fullback, suffered a bad sprain against Atchison last week and is barely able to walk. He has been in sweat clothes all week and is a doubtful starter. His brother Joe may see his first limited action since the opening game of the year when he dislocated an elbow. A cast is still on the arm, however. Bob Stauffer, the third injured back, is in the best shape of the three, although he likely will not be up to par. He also injured an ankle in the Atchison game. Coach Allan Woolard may start an all-underclassmen lineup in the backfield if the situation remains the same. That would put Gary Creamer at quarterback, Bill Smith and Joe Malott at halfbacks and Pete Whitenight at full.

Line in Good Shape

All the line is in good shape with the exception of Wes Walker, who has a sore shoulder. But he should be able to play.

Ragland Rips Jump Record

"What a jump!" declared Dad Perry, as the Tuesday-Thursday fourth hour gym class retired to

An unidentified back is swamped by four Leos in one of the many spectacular plays in the Argentine fray.
The Lions mauled the Mustangs by a score of 33-0.
Lawrence players shown are Wes Walker, William (Junior) Smith, Jerry Cunningham and Lester Smith.

November 13, 1953

Woolardmen Stomp Cyclones; Reap Deadlock With Bulldogs

Hot one minute, cold the next, that was the formula of the Lawrence Lions in their last two gridiron clashes.

The hot end of this pigskin tale came Friday night October 30, when the Woolardmen tamed the Ottawa Cyclones down to a gentle breeze, wolloping them 39-0 on the Cyclone home field. The bright spot of the fray was Terry Malott who had the best night of his career, grinding out a total of 239 yards.

The Cyclones looked as though they were going to give the Leos a rough go of it. Early in the opening stanza the Lions gambled on a fourth down and lost. With Jere Potts doing the quarterbacking the Cyclones rolled to the Lawrence 24, and on the next play from scrimmage Potts faked a pass and rambled to paydirt and a 6-0 lead for the Ottawans. Wes Walker crashed in to block the try for the extra point.

Not satisfied in breaking the gym broadjump record which he accomplished a few weeks ago, Thomas Ragland proceeded to smash the standing high jump record as well.

The feat occurred on Oct. 27, late in the fourth hour period. As Ragland, during his jumping, began to approach the record, "Dad" Perry drew a chalk line across the black board to represent the former records. This was soon topped by Tom as he jumped to a record height of 31 inches. The average for the gym classes is around 21 inches.

One of the most competent Lion gridsters is Wesley Walker, Leo defensive end, who has done a great job of handling his side of the line during this '53 grid season.

Wes, a senior, 173 pound, defensive end, is somewhat different from the rest of the Lion gridsters in that this season is the first in which he has participated in the oval sport.

Wes hasn't competed in any major sports in High School except City League basketball where he donned the title of "Goose" with his exceptionally good ball-handling which pleased the fans to a great extent.

At the beginning of the season, Wes was a familiar stand-out with his vicious tackling and the superb job he accomplished of holding down his end. During the Topeka fray, Wes received a shoulder injury which slowed him down lightly but kept fighting and howed that he still had that initial tamina. In the Ottawa contest,

Walker Holds KO Pace in 3d Armd Div Bouts

HANAU, Germany (Special) — light-heavyweight Wesley Walker continued his sensational knockout pace and four-time division heavyweight champ James Johnson scored a win but these were the only ring victories achieved by the Div Tns Locomotives in bowing to the 3d Armd Div's league-leading CCB Braves, 17-8, here Friday.

Walker continued his undefeated skein by making Harold Malone his fifth straight first-round knockout victim. Malone, who lost once before to Walker in 55 seconds, lasted until the 1:34 mark.

The 222-pound Johnson handed

Willie Carter, 188, his first loss in five starts on a close decision.

Three of CCB's six triumphs came on forfeits with the Div Tns picking up one win via this route. Light-middleweight John Robinson scored the Braves' lone KO, sending Harry Davis down for the count at 1:55 of the second round.

In a special heavyweight bout, CCC's Walter Foster decisioned Div Tns' Alfonso Thames.

The results:
FLYWEIGHT—James Williams, Div' Tns. won on forfeit.
BANTAMWEIGHT — William Garber, CCB, won on forfeit.
FEATHERWEIGHT—Don Ridley, CCB, won on forfeit.
LIGHTWEIGHT — David Jones, CCB, decisioned John Jones.
LIGHT-WELTERWEIGHT — Robert LaVern, CCB, decisioned Wallace Smith.
LIGHT-MIDDLEWEIGHT — John Robinson, CCB, KOd Harry Davis, :55 (2d).
MIDDLEWEIGHT—Leon Noel, CCB, won on forfeit.
LIGHT-HEAVYWEIGHT — Wesley Walker, Div Tns, KOd Harold Malone, 1:34 (1st).
HEAVYWEIGHT—James Johnson, Div Tns, decisioned Willie Carter.

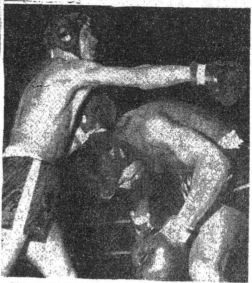

THE MIGHTY MISS—Bill Crockett (right) Div Trans light-heavyweight, may still have been seeing stars if he hadn't ducked this vicious right thrown by Bill Bettis (left), CCA slugger, during Division quarterfinals bout. Bettis did most of

h Armd, VII Corps Pace South Regionals
3d Armd Fighters Feature Northern Bouts

KAISERSLAUTERN, Germany (Special) — A standing-room-only crowd of 1,700 fans was treated to an action-packed program in the USAREUR Northern Regionals as five of nine bouts failed to go the distance at Vogelweh gymnasium Saturday night.

Boxers from the 3d Armd Div grabbed the spotlight in third-round action winning four fights. The 8th Div club scored three victories while the other two were divided Area Comds and V Corps.

Former All Army champ Eddie Cook had another light workout it took him only 2:28 of the round to TKO Booker Anson, V Corps, in a light-midweight go.

The quickest win of the night recorded by 3d Armd Div fight James Johnson. The slugger TKOd D. C. Hale after 1:48 of the first heat.

Sage, DeJesus Win

Lywood Sage, 8th Div, also disposed of his foe in the first round did 8th Div welter Jose DeJesus. Sage knocked out flyweight William Garcer, 3d Armd Div, at :46 mark, while DeJesus KOd Robert Wilkins, Area Comds, :25.

The other bout that failed to go limit was between featherweight Clint Clark, 8th Div, and Earl Gibson, V Corps. Clark knocked out Gibson at 1:50 of the third.

William White, 3d Armd Div lightweight, decisioned L. D. Ludy, Area Comds, while Ricardo Darras, V Corps, copped the nod over Norman Best, 8th Div, in a lighter scrap.

Middleweight Wesley Walker and heavy Willie Carter, both Armd Div, were victorious their encounters. Walker won Garrett, Area Comds, took Joseph Martin, V

AUGSBURG, Germany (Special)—The 4th Armd Div and VII Corps boxing teams set the pace in the final USAREUR Southern Regional card each winning four of nine fights before an overflow crowd of 6,500 at Sheridan gymnasium Saturday night.

The other bout was won by a 7th Army Trps squad. Four of the fights were won by forfeit, while two knockouts were registered.

Light-middleweight Felix Velasquez, VII Corps, and his teammate light-heavy Jerry Harrell both recorded second-round knockouts.

Velasquez put the finisher on Clyde Gillard, 7th Army Trps, at 2:49, while Harrell stopped Com Z' Lester Scott after 2:49 of the round.

Nat Wright was the only 4th Armd Div fighter that had to fight to gain his victory. The other three, featherweight Tom Rainey, lightweight Lonnie Smith and heavyweight Charley Garlington all won via the forfeit route.

Wright decisioned Frank Troxel, VII Corps, in a light-welter affair.

Willis Jackson, VII Corps welter and teammate Joe Biggers, a heavyweight, both won their matches. Jackson copped the verdict over Tom Herset, 7th Army Trps, while Biggers bested Matt Hill, 24th Div, heavyweight.

Light-middleweight Willie Young, 7th Army Trps, also won his fight by forfeit.

The results:
FEATHERWEIGHT—Tom Rainey, 4th Armd Div, won by forfeit over James High, 7th Army Trps.
LIGHTWEIGHT—Lonnie Smith, 4th Armd Div, won by forfeit over Joe Ruffino, VII Corps.
LIGHT-WELTERWEIGHT—Nat Wright, 4th Armd Div, decisioned Frank Troxel, VII Corps.
WELTERWEIGHT—Willis Jackson, VII Corps, decisioned Tom Herset, 7th Army Trps.
LIGHT-MIDDLEWEIGHT—Willie Young, 7th Army Trps, won by forfeit over Al Harris, VII Corps.
MIDDLEWEIGHT — Felix Velasquez, VII Corps, KOd Clyde Gillard, 7th Army Trps.

The results:
FLYWEIGHT—Lywood Sage, 8th Div, KOd William Garcer, 3d Armd Div, 2:46 (1st).
FEATHERWEIGHT—Clint Clark, 8th Div, KOd Earl Gibson, V Corps 1:50 (3d).
LIGHTWEIGHT—William White, 3d Armd Div, decisioned L. D. Ludy, Area Comds.
LIGHT-WELTERWEIGHT—Ricardo Darras, V Corps, decisioned Norman Best, 8th Div.
WELTERWEIGHT—Jose DeJesus, 8th Div, TKOd Robert Wilkins, Area Comds, 2:25.
LIGHT-MIDDLEWEIGHT—Eddie Crook, Area Comds, TKOd Booker Anderson, V Corps, 2:28 (1st).
MIDDLEWEIGHT—Wesley Walker, 3d Armd Div, decisioned Vernon Garrett, Area Comds.
LIGHT-HEAVYWEIGHT—Willie Carter, 3d Armd Div, decisioned Joseph Martin, V Corps.
HEAVYWEIGHT—James Johnson, 3d Armd Div, TKOd D. C. Hale, 8th Div, 1:48 (1st).

Nat'l AAU Tourn

r-Old Captures
. Championship

By RON AMOS
R-J Sports Editor

ez, a 16-year-old Junior high school
uston, Tex., is the sensation of the
: Union boxing world today.

led his way to the 147-pound champ-
964 National AAU Senior Boxing
riday night at Convention Center
d even further by being named the
standing fighter.

er won an
intercolle-
tin (Skip)
afternoon
back to
upset in
r Quincy
Force, a
n the 1960
ome.

a feat for
st appear-
urnament.
Valdez is
been box-
years old
e way he
experienc-

as a mat-
nd boxing

the three-
he Michi-

— Will Cross of Portland
TKO'd Robert McMillian of Toledo to capture the 165-pound
crown. McMillian won the Gold-
en Gloves title in that division.

— Hard-hitting Toby Gibson
of Spokane cut up Pete Esquibel of Clovis, N. M., in the
156-pound final, winning a second-round TKO.

— Freddie Ward of Portland
decisioned Tom Davis of Salt
Lake City to annex 139-pound
laurels.

— In the 132-pound class,
Ron Harris of Detroit outpoint-
ed Herb Dallison of Washington
D. C.

— Charles Brown of the
Marines won a second-round
TKO over Pete Spanakos of
New York City for the 125-
pound title when Spanakos
suffered a cut over his right
eye.

MARSH BOWS TO GIANT

James Beattie, 245-Pounder Who Stands 6-Feet-7, Twices Floors K. U. Football Player to Win Gloves Heavyweight Bout.

LEFT HAND PACKS MOST PUNCH

Both Trips to Canvas Come as Result of Southpaw Blows—Ronnie Can't Get Inside Enough.

RCH 1, 1962.

By Paul O'Boynick.
(A Member of The Star's Sports Staff.)

Chicago, Feb. 28.—Ronnie Marsh, Kansas City heavyweight, put up a spirited battle against size and experience tonight only to lose to James Beattie, Minnesota giant, before 6,000 howling fans in the Western National Golden Gloves at the Chicago stadium.

The 6-foot, 8-inch 24-pounder, who is appearing in his third tournament here, twice floored Marsh.

The first knockdown came in the first round as the result of a slashing left hand. When Ronnie tried to break through the long reach of Beattie, Marsh went down on one knee and popped right back up, but the referee made the University of Kansas football player take the mandatory 8-count.

Beattie not only employed slashing left, but he would follow it with effective rights.

Ronnie had a cut over his right eye and a mouse under his right eye. Ronnie came back strong, however, as he tried to get in close to land punches, but the big boy either would hold or step away.

Marsh tried to retaliate as he moved in quickly near the close of the opening stanza and landed solid short punches.

The Jaywaker roared back in the second round and it appeared that he might wipe out that knockdown.

Ronnie Too Eager.

But carelessness cost him. Beattie again whipped across another stinging left and that sent Ronnie reeling to the canvas. He recuperated rapidly and was up on his feet at the count of three. Marsh took advantage of a longer rest as the timekeeper dogged the count to eight.

Then Ronnie's best punch, a short left, caught Beattie flush on the nose and sent him back on his heels. The referee warned Beattie for holding and near the end of the second stanza Marsh staged another spurt that forced the giant to cover up. Both fighters tired rapidly as the bell ended the round.

Ronnie stalked his foe at the beginning of the final round. He knew he had to score a knockout to win.

Beattie's Reach Helps.

Each time Marsh charged into the big fellow, Beattie would tie him up with his octopus-like arms.

A hard left hand by Marsh landed on the chin of Beattie, and it draped him over the top rope. Marsh, sensing the Minnesotan was in trouble, started a 2-fisted attack and again Beattie slipped out of it by hugging him fiercely with his long reach.

TWO RING KINGS FACE BIG TASKS

Potent Foes Stand in Paths of Thurnell Thompson and Frank House.

Feb 1961

FINAL NIGHT FOR GLOVES

Municipal Auditorium Program Includes 28 Bouts —Starts at 8.

By Paul O'Boynick.
(A Member of The Star's Sports Staff.)

The only two defending Golden Gloves champions, Thurnell Thompson, lightweight, and Frank House, heavyweight, realize they will face some keen competition in tonight's final program at the Municipal Auditorium.

Starting at 8 o'clock, there will be 28 bouts—12 semifinal and eight final open division and eight final novice scraps. These conclude the 26th annual Tournament of Champions.

Thompson must sidetrack Gerald Box, Algoa, for the right to meet the winner of the Claude Samson-Joe Brown event for the crown. House's first foe will be Raford Wilson, Pan-American. The other heavies are Delroy Faust, Miami, Okla., and Roy Rodreques, Pan-American.

Box Has Speed.

While Thurnell is a ringwise veteran with a solid punch, Box will rely on speed and clever boxing in hopes of staging an upset.

The Samson-Brown go stacks up as anybody's fight.

Samson also will be seeking his second lightweight crown. The 24-year-old Maryville

Special Trophies for Golden Gloves.

Special trophies will be presented tonight to the winners of flyweight, lightheavy and heavyweight divisions in the Golden Gloves Tournament of Champions at the Municipal Auditorium.

The Beebe Rich Memorial trophy will go to the winning 112-pounder. The heavy champion will receive the Kansas City police department trophy. There will also be a hustle award, best sportsman and outstanding boxer trophy.

State college senior who is majoring in physical education, took the 135-pound title two years ago.

Brown not only can go at full speed but he is one of the stiffest punchers in the lightweight division. Only 18, Brown apparently has copied Floyd Patterson's style. He arches his neck like the heavyweight king and throws punches in the same manner.

Although Jewell Shane and Buster Talley are picked to win their semifinal bouts from Esto Jackson, Gateway, and Cleveland Owens, Algoa, in the order named, anything can happen. Shane and Talley are fighters. They are willing to take a punch if it gives them an opening to counter. Shane relies on a left hook and follows it up with a hard right.

Never Eases Up.

Talley is definitely the "fightingest fighter" in the tournament. He throws leather constantly and swarms all over his opponent.

The all-Gateway final between Wesley Walker and Sam Watson should be a thriller.

Watson will be shooting for his second straight championship. Last year Sam walked off with the 160-pound title and moved up to the 175-pound class this year.

Walker and Watson are mean punchers. Walker exhibited his hitting prowess by defeating Preston Thomas, lightheavy champ, in the semifinals Wednesday night, while Watson took care of Joe Rollins, 1959 lightheavy crown bearer.

Watson is 27 and Walker is 24. This bout could go either way.

Walter Allen of Pan-American is highly touted in the featherweight open. The little fellow has plenty of steam behind his punches. His foe in the semifinals will be Ronald McConnell, a stablemate. Carroll Yeubanks, Coffeyville, Kas., and Larry Sampel, St. Benedict's, will swap punches in the other 126-pound semifinal bout.

The eight winners in the open division will represent Kansas City in the Western national late this month in the Chicago stadium.

INTEREST IS UP ON HEAVY BOUT

Ronnie Marsh to Meet Ray Love in Golden Gloves Clash Tonight.

BIG PROGRAM ON TAP

Municipal Auditorium Will Be Scene of 42 Fights Beginning at 7 o'Clock.

By Paul O'Boynick.
(A Member of The Star's Sports Staff.)

Most of the interest will be focused tonight on the Ronnie Marsh-Ray Love heavyweight bout in the Golden Gloves Tournament of Champions at the Municipal Auditorium. A total of 42 bouts will be on the program, starting at 7 o'clock.

Marsh, guard on the University of Kansas freshman team, will meet a formidable opponent in the Joplin, Mo. belter, who stands 6-1 and weighs 200 pounds. Marsh is a 192-pound, 6-footer.

Three More Slated.

Three more heavy bouts will be on the card with Frank House starting defense of his title against Randy Ojeda, Don Bosco club. Joe Bradford, former University of Houston student, takes on Rayford Wilson and Roy Rodriquez oppose Don Cippola.

Bradford, a computer operator in the Army who is stationed at Pleasant Hill, Mo., is competing in the open for the first time. Four years ago, he won the novice championship in Houston.

If the pattern continues, the three remaining defending champions may join Thurnell Thompson, defeated lightweight king, on the sidelines.

The three remaining titlists are Jewell Shane, welterweight; Wesley Walker, light heavyweight and House.

Golden Gloves Pairings.

Order of Bouts.
QUARTER FINALS.
NOVICE DIVISION.
126-POUND CLASS.
1—Cecil Allen, Northland, vs. Cornelius Strong, Argentine.
2—Joe Vaughn, Gateway, vs. Harry Rayton, Lawrence, Kas.
3—Ray Newton, Argentine, vs. Dino Haskins, Whatsoever Boys club.
4—Jesse Hurtado, Don Bosco, vs. James Roper, Pan American.
160-POUND CLASS.
5—John Delgardo, Don Bosco, vs. Terry Allen Graham, Whatsoever Boys club.
OPEN DIVISION
126-POUND CLASS.
6—Larry Sampel, Pan American, vs. James Collins, Algoa, Jefferson City.
7—Tommy Brown, Coffeyville, Kas., vs. David Stuckey, Argentine Parish House.
147-POUND CLASS.
8—Jewell Shane, Whatsoever Boys club, vs. Sylvester Johnson, Joplin, Mo.
9—Estelle Jackson, Gateway, vs. Myron Nevelles, Argentine Parish House.
10—Terry Aleshire, Pan American, vs. Ronnie Douglas, Coffeyville, Kas.
11—Ronald McConnell, Pan American, vs. Carl Bolden, Argentine Parish House.
160-POUND CLASS.
12—Terry Allen, Pan American, vs. Robert Howard, Gateway.
13—Buster Talley, Whatsoever Boys club, vs. Edgar Bradford, Columbia, Mo.
14—Anthony Bowman, Gateway, vs. Ross Whitemen, Whatsoever Boys club.
15—David Smith, Leavenworth, Kas., vs. Charles Adams, Pan American.
Heavyweight Class.
16—Ray Love, Joplin, Mo., vs. Ronnie Marsh, Lawrence, Kas.

Tough Shane Foe.

Shane meets a tough foe in Sylvester Johnson, Joplin, Mo. Sylvester, a classy boxer with a terrific punch, may rely on skill and speed to dethrone Shane. Johnson stopped the ring streak of Cleveland Owens, Algoa, at 10 in a row last night with adept boxing. Shane is strictly a slugger although he has one of the best hooks in the tournament.

Walker, who won the 175-pound title last year by knocking out Sam Watson, meets the same foe tonight.

These two stablemates put up a spirited battle last year until Walker set him up with a right hand that sent him to the canvas for the victory.

Here's Another.

Another bout that may keep the fans on the edge of their seats will be waged between Walt Allen, Pan-Am lightweight, and Douglas Wickward, Joplin, Mo. Allen showed tremendous punching ability last night in soundly thrashing Cecil Battles. Allen is seeking his third title in as many divisions in three years. He is the former featherweight and bantam king.

Joe Penalis, Coffeyville,

17—Joe Bradford, Whatsoever Boys club vs. Rayford Wilson, Pan American.
18—Roy Rodriquez, Pan American vs. Don Cipolla, Whatsoever Boys club.
19—Randy Ojeda, Don Bosco, vs. Frank House, Gateway.

Semifinals.
112-pound Class.
20—Arus Gunnels, Gateway, vs. William Conway, Pan American.
118-pound Class.
21—Herman Bowman, Algoa, Jefferson City, vs. Bernard Jenkins, Pan American.
22—Harry Fullard, Coffeyville, Kas., vs. John Lattimore, Gateway.
135-pound Class.
23—Walter Allen, Pan American, vs. Douglass Wickware, Joplin, Mo.
24—Donald McIntosh, Y. M. C. A., vs. Joe Penolis, Coffeyville, Kas.
175-pound Class.
25—Cordell Ricks, Joplin, Mo., vs. Paul Holder, Whatsoever Boys club.
26—Wesley Walker, Gateway, vs. Sam Watson, Gateway.

NOVICE DIVISION.
112-pound Class.
27—Wally Warfield, Argentine, vs. Franklin Anderson, Pan American.
28—Cleveland Ford, Gateway, vs. Donnie Spencer, Joplin, Mo.
118-pound Class.
29—Arthur Hardy, Whatsoever Boys club vs. Dwight Horion, Pan American.
30—Adie Horton, Pan American, vs. Michael Smith, Gateway.
126-Pound Class.
31—Winner, Allen-Strong vs. winner, Vaugn-Rayton.
32—Winner, Newton-Haskins vs. winner, Hurtado-Roper.
135-Pound Class.
33—Jerry Campbell, Whatsoever Boys club, vs. Carv Watson, Joplin Mo
34—Ellington Bell, Pan American, vs. Ronald Diver, Cameron, Police club.
147-Pound Class.
35—Troy Carson, Whatsoever Boys club, vs. Jerry Wright, Pan American.
36—Bob Taverpoero, Whatsoever Boys club, vs. Emery Peterson, Lawrence, Kas.
160-Pound Class.
37—Winner, Delgardo-Graham vs. Robert Lowe, Gateway.
38—Carl Tracy, Coffeyville, Kas., vs. Willie Jones, Pan American.
175-Pound Class.
39—Andrew Gray, Argentine Parish house, vs. Charles Walker, Lawrence.
40—Jeffrey Merritt, Pan American, vs. Russell McDorkey, Cameron, Police club.
OPEN DIVISION.
126-Pound Class.
41—Winner, Sampel-Collins vs. winner, Brown-Stuckey.
42—John Dorcy, Northland, vs. Charles Garrison, Gateway.

Kas., mauler who eliminated Thompson's chances of a repeat championship in the 135-pound class, is matched with Donald McIntosh, Y. M. C. A. southpaw. Penalis is a strong boxer and continually wades in against his opponents.

Most of the experts believe Allen and Penalis are the classiest in the lightweight class.

Penalis is a slow starter who picks up momentum as he goes along.

Buster Talley also makes his debut as a middleweight. Talley, a finalist in the welter last year, had put on weight and his coach, Vern Gregory, believes he will be much stronger in the 160-pound division.

93

K. U. Gridder Eyes Ring Title.

JANUARY 28, 1962.

By Paul O'Boynick.
(A Member of The Star's Sports Staff.)

RONNIE MARSH, an outstanding guard on the University of Kansas freshman football team, is making a ring comeback at 19 years of age.

The 6-foot 190-pounder will make a strong bid for the heavyweight title in the 27th annual Golden Gloves Tournament of Champions, February 6, 7 and 10 in the Municipal Auditorium.

Ronnie was only 12 years old when he first put on the gloves in a ring. He won the flyweight title in the novice division of the 1956 Kansas City, Kansas, Gloves tourney. The next year he competed as a welterweight and won the city championship. He was runner-up in the state. He quit boxing until this season. He will represent Lawrence, Kas., in the annual tourney here.

Diving Title, Too.

In addition to football, track and boxing, Marsh captured the 1959 Kansas state diving championship as a junior at Wyandotte.

Ronnie played football for Coach Ed Ellis at guard, fullback and left half as a sophomore. He moved up to a starting role as a junior at both guard and left half. Elected captain in his senior year, he quit school when he was ruled out of all extra-curricular activities.

After leaving Wyandotte in 1959, Marsh enlisted in the Marines and cleared boot camp. However, he was released from the service when it was discovered that he was under age.

When his family moved to Omaha, where his father, Milford S. Marsh, is employed in a packing plant, Ronnie enrolled at Omaha Tech high school where he engaged in both football and swimming.

FROM PADS TO GLOVES—Ronnie Marsh, a guard on Kansas's freshman football team, will be one of the favorites in the heavyweight division of the Golden Gloves Tournament of Champions next month at the Municipal Auditorium.

In the grid sport he earned recognition as an all-state guard and also won the Nebraska state diving title. As a pole vaulter he cleared the bar at 13 feet, one inch.

Marsh is regarded as one of the best heavyweights to enter the tournament here since Tony Novak, sensational heavyweight who won successive titles in 1938-39 and went on to win every national amateur heavyweight crown. Ronnie, a terrific puncher, will be the favorite, although Frank House of the Gateway Athletic club, will be shooting for his third straight title in the heavy division.

Ready for Football.

"I just want to see f I can go through the heavy class," Ronnie said about his return to the ring. "Boxing also is helping me to stay in condition for football."

Many who have seen Ronnie in the ring, predict the youngster can go all the way in the Tournament of Champions because of his terrific punching ability. He appears to be at his best when the going gets tough.

Charles Myers, director of the annual tournament, is high on the youngster.

"That guy (Marsh) can hit," Myers observed. "He is in excellent condition. It will be the first time in several years that we will have some strong contenders in the heavy division. He has real co-ordination and many Kansas City, Kansas, patrons will be rooting for him to take the crown."

Others on the Lawrence, Kas., ring list who will compete include Pete Russell, 175; Gary Thomas, 160; Harry Rayton and Byron Hurst, lightweights.

Wesley Walker, defending light heavyweight champion, representing Gateway A. C., also is a Lawrence, Kas., ring product. Walker made a great showing in the Chicago stadium last February.

Shane, Walker Open Bidding In Ring Meet

By Paul O'Boynick.
(A Member of The Star's Sports Staff.)

CHICAGO, Feb. 28—Jewell Shane and Wesley Walker, regarded as the bright hopes on the Kansas City boxing team, will get their tests tonight as the ringmen in the heavier classes see action for the first time in the Western National in the Chicago stadium.

Shane, a welterweight, and Wesley, a lightheavy, who are willing to trade a punch to shoot across a jolting right or left, are eager for competition as are Ken Maples, middleweight, and Frank House, a heavyweight.

Foes in Doubt.

The Kansas City fighters don't know yet who their opponents will be, but they don't seem to be worried. The four Kansas Citians must weigh in at noon today and then pass physical examinations before the first round pairings are made.

Competition will be extremely tough in the heavier classes.

The only defending champion is Leotis Martin, Toledo, middleweight.

Julius Garcia, Denver, is highly regarded in the 160-pound division.

Garcia was a finalist in the lightheavy class last year, bowing to Jeff Davis. Since last year, however, Garcia has scaled down to the middleweight division and he is picked by the experts to go a long way.

Satisfied Despite Losses.

But anything can happen in this tournament and Kansas City coaches are hopeful the bigger boys will give a good account of themselves. Bubbles Klice, Vern Gregory and Joey Aguilar were more than satisfied with the showing of the youngsters last night in the lighter classes.

Although Allen Lattimore was the only winner last night, Klice pointed out that Thurnell Thompson, Walter Allen and Jerry Sampel did right well in a losing cause.

Thompson appeared to hold the edge early in his fight with Wayne Mundy, Nashville, Tenn., but the Kansas City boy didn't follow up his chances. Twice in the second and third rounds Thurnell seemed to have Mundy in distress, but the Dixie fighter, who held a longer reach, pecked away with his left and came 'ack with true right hand jolts to gain the verdict.

Allen couldn't break through Joe Bennett's defense in a 126-pound bout, while Sampel's lack of experience cost him his bout with Leroy Romero.

Wesley Walker Is Eliminated After Taking 1st Flight

Wesley Walker of Lawrence, fighting for the Kansas City Golden Gloves team, Tuesday night won his first fight in the Tournament of Champions at Chicago, but lost in his second bid and is eliminated.

Walker decisioned Leo Peters of Cedar Rapids in his first light heavyweight bout, then dropped a three-round verdict to Billy Newsom of Detroit.

This marked Walker's first appearance in the Chicago ring, although he had won in Kansas City previously.

Fighters winning their second bout Thursday advanced to the semifinals of the Chicago action.

Won't Fight His Kid Brother—and Doesn't

BY FRANK MASTRO

Wesley Walker saved Leo Peters from the embarrassment of meeting his younger brother, John, in last night's light heavyweight competition in the Golden Gloves Tournament of Champions in Chicago Stadium.

Walker, Kansas City representative, eliminated Leo, 28 year old former University of Iowa halfback, on a three round decision in their first round bout.

Meanwhile, Johnng Peters, 22 year old senior at Corpus Christi university, was qualifying for his second round contest by scoring a third round technical knockout over Bert Bailey of Des Moines, also at 175 pounds.

"I won't fight my kid brother, no matter what," Leo said before he entered the ring against Walker, 24 year old Lawrence, Kas., army dischargee who went all the way to the semi-finals last year.

LOCAL GLOVERS WAIT FOR BELL

Lighter Weights See Action Tonight in Chicago Tournament of Champions.

PAIRINGS READY TODAY

Tomorrow Night's Cards Sends Shane, Maples, Walker, House Into Ring.

By Paul O'Boynick.
(A Member of The Star's Sports Staff.)

Chicago, Feb. 26.—Kansas City boxers are ready to toss their best punches in first round Western national Golden Gloves action tomorrow night at the Chicago stadium.

The program, starting at 7 o'clock, will bring into action all of the 112, 118, 126 and 185-pounders. Representing Kansas City in the lighter weights are flyweight Allen Lattimore, bantam Walt Allen, featherweight Jerry Sampel and lightweight Thurnell Thompson.

These fighters will be weighed-in and given physical examinations starting at noon. Pairings will be made about 3 o'clock tomorrow afternoon.

Twenty-eight out-of-town centers will have strong representatives in the event.

Tuesday program calls for the appearance of the boxers in the other four weight classes, while, on Wednesday, the winners of bouts tomorrow night and Tuesday night will return in all weights.

Other Kansas Citians who will enter the ring Tuesday night include welter Jewell Shane, middleweight Ken Maples, lightheavy Wesley Walker and heavyweight Frank House.

Coaches Bubbles Klice, Vern Gregory and Joey Aguilar accompanied the team here.

"Getting past the first bout is all-important," Klice said. "It gives a boy more confidence. Our kids are ready to make a good showing."

Two of the stiffest punchers on the Kansas City squad are Shane and Walker. Three others, Thompson, Allen and House have had experience in the Chicago tourney. Both Thompson and Allen are engaging in their second tournament, while House is a 3-time performer here.

Shane and Walker were the sensations of the Kansas City 3-day grind. Both, however, will face some rugged competition.

The heavyweight title is wide open this year since Cassius Clay of Louisville will not compete.

Clay won the heavy crown last year and wound up taking the Olympic gold medal in the lightheavy class in Rome. He's since turned pro and is a sparring mate for Ingemar Johannson.

Louisville, however, will have a potent 1-2 punch. Teaming with James Ellis, last year's finalist in the middleweight division, is Lawrence Howard, a lightheavy, who twice won the all-Navy championship and has scored a record of 62 victories in 66 fights.

Ellis did not permit an opponent to get past the second round in his first four fights last year, but in the 160-pound championship bout he lost the decision to Leotis Martin of Toledo, who also is After appearing in the Intercity bouts at Madison Square Garden, Ellis won the lightheavy crown in the Olympic trials held in Louisville and then dropped a split verdict to Wilbert McClure, Toledo, in the San Francisco finals. McClure, a former Chicago champion from Ohio, went on to win a gold medal in Rome.

Monday, February 27, 1961.

Westvaco and Walker's Gain City League Wins

Westvaco turned back Walt's 58-53, in City League basketball Wednesday night at the Community Building. In the second game, Walker's handled Haskell, 62-40.

H. Hines was high for Westvaco with 15, while Roger Hill got 17 the losers. Charlie Thurston scored 22 to pace Walker's against Haskell and H. Whitehat got 14 for the losers.

Friday's schedule: 7 p.m., Teepee-10-40 vs. VFW and 8:30, DeSoto vs Carbaugh's.

GLOVERS FADE IN WINDY CITY

Wesley Walker, Only Kansas City Boxer to Win Bout, Then Bows Out.

OTHERS LOSE IN HURRY

Jewell Shane, Kenneth Maples and Frank House Go Out in First Matches.

By Paul O'Boynick.
(A Member of The Star's Sports Staff.)

Chicago, Feb. 28.—Wesley Walker, Kansas City light heavyweight, gave it all he had tonight only to lose a heartbreaking decision to Billy Newsome, Detroit machinist, in the second round of the Western National Golden Gloves at Chicago stadium.

The three other Kansas Citians in the heavier divisions, Jewell Shane, welter; Kenneth Maples, middleweight, and Frank House, heavyweight, were eliminated in the first round.

Shane was defeated by Richard Gilford, Chicago; Maples was outpointed by C. B. Smith, Kenosha, Wis., and House lost to Phil Browner, Muncie, Ind.

Walker gained the right to meet Newsome with a triumph over Leo Peters, Cedar Rapids, Ia., 175-pounder. Walker was ahead all the way and came within an eyelash of scoring a second round knockout with a terrific left hook to the stomach of the Iowan. The bell sounded at the toll of nine, saving Peters.

Crowd Booes Verdict.

The crowd of approximately 7,000 fans warmed up to the Walker-Newsome bout, best of the night.

The decision could have gone either way. It was that close although fans booed for more than two minutes after Newsome was announced as the winner.

Wesley uncorked a short right in the last two minutes that knocked Newsome's mouthpiece to the fifth row of ringside seats. Newsome bloodied Walker's nose in the second round.

Shane didn't win a round against Gilford, a highly polished boxer. Realizing that he was far behind, in the second round, Shane began to shoot the works and his hard right rocked Gilford.

Timing Switch Made.

Maples' timing was bad in his loss to C. B. Smith of Kenosha. Everything that Maples tried appeared to backfire.

In the second found Kenneth changed his tactics and went into the unorthodox southpaw style. This didn't help either.

Although House forced the fight virtually all the way against Phil Browner, there wasn't too much force behind House's blows and Browner would counter with looping rights and lefts. House was by far the better boxer but Browner landed the harder punches.

FIRST ROUND.
147-POUND CLASS — Richard Gilford, Chicago, dec. Jewell Shane, Kansas City.
160-POUND CLASS—C. B. Smith, Kenosha, Wis., dec. Kenneth Maples, Kansas City.
175-POUND CLASS — Wesley Walker, Kansas City, dec. Leo Peters, Cedar Rapids, Ia.
HEAVYWEIGHT CLASS—Phil Browner, Muncie, Ind., dec. Frank House, Kansas City.

SECOND ROUND.
175-POUND CLASS — Billy Newsome, Dec. Wesley Walker.

96

Local Boxers Dominate Chicago Gloves Entry

By Paul O'Boynick
(A Member of The Star's Sports Staff.)

FOR the first time in more than 20 years, Kansas City will have virtually a home-town team in the Western National Golden Gloves Tournament of Champions. The 1961 event starts tomorrow night at the Chicago stadium.

Seven of the swingers are local men—Allen Lattimore, Walt Allen, Jerry Sampel, Thurnell Thompson, Jewell Shane, Ken Maples and Frank House.

The eighth member is Wesley Walker, lightheavyweight, who lives in Lawrence, Kas., but will wear the colors of the Gateway club in the Chicago event.

Allen, Thompson and House have been in the Chicago tournament before and the experience should help them. Allen and Thompson will be appearing in their second tourney, while House is competing for the third time in the heavyweight class.

Both Allen and Thompson are smooth boxers and each packs a wallop. Thompson, at 28, has a fine amateur ring record.

Jewell Shane and Wesley Walker, welter and lightheavyweight, respectively, could be the biggest surprises on the Kansas City team.

They are punchers capable of stopping any foe they hit. Shane employs a rugged left hook. Walker proved to be one of the outstanding 2-fisted punchers in the tournament here.

Back in 1938, eight Kansas Citians captured titles in the Municipal Auditorium. Members of that squad included the late Beebe Rich, flyweight; Chester Ellis, 118; Jackie Simmons, 126; Harry Nills, 135; Ray McDonald, 147; Terry Nolan, 160; Louis Jackson, lightheavy, and Tony Novak, heavyweight.

Golden Gloves Champions

garoo jab and then got tied up with a nifty arm lock by Thomas. He fell victim to a right clout in the third and even after being revived, had that "what am I doing here?" look.

Another popular favorite came to the end of the line, sudden like. Richard Riley, Ward high gridder, gave his cheering section just about fifty seconds of happiness as he tore into Jerome Seaman, transplanted North Carolinan. Riley made the mistake of leading with his left once too often.

Seaman stepped in and—as Riley said when he came to," "What hit me?" Even so the young Irishman is tabbed a comer and no doubt will be entered in the novice division of the Tournament of Champions next week in Municipal auditorium.

Ropes were a hazard, or a godsend, depending on who you were rooting for. Delbert Kimbrough, Sumner football star and 160-pound novice winner, put Mike Zuricak, Whatsoever, thru the ropes in the third round and floored that worthy in the first. Richard Davenport of Lawrence sent his fellow townsman, Lawrence Rebick, sprawling thru the ropes in the 175-pound novice scrap but the latter gave him a bloody nose in retaliation.

Another real blood and thunder scrap was the 175-pound open meeting between Preston Thomas of Argentine and Wesley Walker of Lawrence. Thomas went down for the 4-count in the first and Walker hit the deck in the second but Thomas ran out of gas in the third and Walker quickly ended it in thirty-seven seconds.

William Harlin, Argentine, was a victim of a split decision in the 135-pound open while Ruben Anaya, Skyline, was the beneficiary of a split decision in the 126-pound novice.

The results:

NOVICE CLASS FINALS

135 pounds—Ernest Mitchell, Argentine Parish house, won by default from John Gonzales, Skyline.
135 pounds—Earl Sutton, Sumner, won by a technical knockout in thirty seconds from Ira Brown, Skyline.
135 pounds (championship)—Sutton won a split decision from Mitchell.
112 pounds—Don Cutchow, Sumner A. C. won the decision from Claude Pingleton, Whatsoever Boys club.
118 pounds—Curtis Maupin, Whatsoever won by a technical knockout in the third round from William White, Argentine.
126 pounds—Ruben Anaya, Skyline won a split decision from Maurice Brown, Springhill.
147 pounds—Jerome Seaman, Whatsoever, stopped Richard Riley, Argentine, in thirty seconds.
160 pounds—Delbert Kimbrough won by a technical knockout in the third round from Mike Zuricak, Whatsoever.
175 pounds — Richard Davenport, Lawrence, won by decision from Lawrence Rebick, Lawrence.
Heavyweight — William Burnison, Lawrence, won by a technical knockout in twenty-five seconds from Richard Scott, Argentine.

OPEN CLASS FINALS

112 pounds—Clifford Hayes, Whatsoever, won by default from Eddie Chow, Argentine.
118 pounds—Jerry Morales, Whatsoever, won by default from Joe Chow, Argentine.
Overweight exhibition—Morales won by decision from Hayes.
126 pounds—Ernie Boulware, Whatsoever, won by decision from Emmett Tucker, Argentine.

Thursday Evening, February 7, 1957.

by Green Ringmen

Winners last night in the Kansas City Kansas Golden Gloves tournament display their "loot." Open champions were given trunks and robes. Runnersup received medals and in addition trophies were given to outstanding boxers.

Top quarter of open champions are, Clifford Hayes, Whatsoever, 112; Jerry Morales, Whatsoever, 118; Ernie Boulware, Whatsoever, 126; and John Benison, Whatsoever, 135 pounds.

Second group includes Wardell Banks, Argentine Parish house, 147; Buster Talley, Whatsoever, 160 pound; Wesley Walker, Lawrence, 175, and Alonzo Thomas, Argentine, heavyweight.

Four heavier weight champions in the novice division: Jerome Seaman, Whatsoever, 147; Delbert Kimbrough, Sumner, 160; Richard Davenport, Lawrence, 175 and William Burnison, Lawrence, heavyweight.

In the bottom panel the "little" men pose for the photographer: Don Cutchow, Sumner, 112; Curtis Maupin, Whatsoever, 118; Ruben Anaya, Skyline, 126; and Earl Sutton Sumner, 135. (Kansas

(photos by Art McGowan)

Other Local Golden Glovers for 1962

KU freshman footballer Ron Marsh is the best-known member of the 1962 Lawrence Golden Gloves team sponsored by the Jaycees. Marsh fights in Kansas City tonight for an open heavyweight title and was pictured earlier this week in the Journal-World. Here is the rest of the Lawrence team: Front row (left to right)—Mike Wood, 1309 Ky. St., and Gary Rayton, 221 Ill. St. Back row (left to right)—Emery Peterson, 516 N 7th St.; Everett Estelle, 629 N. 7th St.; Charles Walker Jr., 501 Fla. St.; coach Howard Walker. Peterson also fights in Kansas City tonight for the title in the 147-pound novice class. Marsh also helped Walker coach the team and in addition to being a promising boxer and KU footballer, Marsh was an outstanding swimming diver during his high school career in Kansas City and Omaha. (Journal-World P

Marsh Reigns After T.K.O.

FEBRUARY 11, 1962.

THE devastating punches of Ronnie Marsh brought him the Golden Gloves heavyweight championship last night before an estimated 6,500 fans in the Municipal Auditorium, when the University of Kansas freshman football player stopped Frank House, 2-time defending champion, in the first round.

The end for House came in 1:55 when referee Ray Sissom brought a halt to the fight after Marsh handed out severe punishment to the Gateway boxer.

House was on the canvas twice for mandatory counts of eight, result of pounding lefts and rights.

Ronnie brought the crowd to its feet early when he cut loose with a barrage of punches. He jolted House twice, then sent him to the deck with a loping left to the jaw. A few seconds later, Marsh staged another of his lightning-offenses and again had house in trouble.

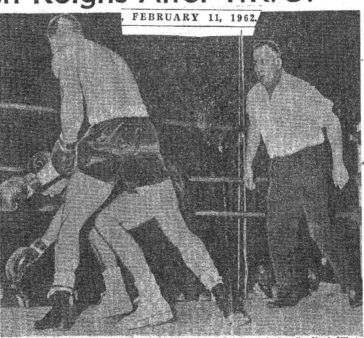

GOING DOWN—Ronnie Marsh of Lawrence, Kas., pounds Joe Bradford, What-... ... Golden Gloves. Bradford starts ... Marsh won

Sunday, February 18, 1962

★ ★ ★ ★ ★ ★

Wichitans Win 4 Go

K-Stat
Wichita Rallies
To Nail Vict...

Yeubanks Top Two Divisions

By JIM KELTNER
Eagle Sports Writer

Wichita placed four fighters on the 1962 Kansas Golden Gloves team Saturday night at the Forum in the 35th annual state tournament.

Whirlwind Wes Walker looked very impressive in winning the 175-pound title scoring a technical knockout over two-time champion Jerry Cline of Liberal, Kan. Walker used a rushing type of attack which completely dazed and bewildered the former champion.

The fighting Yeubanks brothers of Wichita took two of the eight spots on the team. Twin brothers Carol and Gene won their Class A bouts while another brother, Bob, won in the novice ranks.

Gene scored a mild upset over 1960 National runner-up Harold Wilson, Great Bend, Kan., in the 126-pound class.

Carol decisioned Henry Fullard, Coffeyville, Kan., for the 118-pound crown.

Wellington, Kan., placed two fighters on the team. Alex Hernandez won the 112-pound title while defending heavyweight champion John Ledesma beat his old rival from Liberal, Kan., Billy Beck.

Ledesma used a powerful right hand in banging his way to the heavyweight crown, pounding Beck with thundering body blows and staggering the Liberal fighter with rights to the head.

WAC Tops 'B'-Class

Wichita fighters completely dominated the novice fights winning all matches but two. Harry Neal of Coffeyville, Kan., won the 118-pound class and Paul Carnjo of Wellington took the heavyweight title unopposed.

Wichita Athletic Club took wins in five of the matches while Vern Millers Boys Club of Wichita took three events.

One of the more humorous events took place in the 160-pound novice class when Tom Carlyle of Liberal and Willard Woods of Wichita each connected with solid right hands. The result was both boys landed on the seat of their pants at the same time. The crowd, as well as referee Chet Cook, howled with laughter.

Tom Lutkie rallied to decision Neil Edwards of Hutchinson in one of the better bouts of the Novice Class.

Oscar Batts fighting for Vern Miller's Boys club scored a tko over Roger Norris in ...
wild and woolly affair...

CLASS A CHAMPIONSHIP RESULTS
112 pound—Alex Hernandez. Wellington, dec. Hank Cordova, Liberal.
118 pounds — Carol Eubank, Wac, dec. Henry Fullard, Coffeyville.
126 pounds — Gene Eubanks, WAC, dec. Harold Wilson, Great Bend.
135 pounds—Doug Wickware, WAC, tko'ed Oadis Ivory, Newkirk, Okla.
147 pounds—Ivan Page, Hutchinson, dec. Jim Woods, Blackwell, Okla.
160 pounds—Les Elbert, Blackwell, Okla., dec. Damon Ricks, Coffeyville.
175 pounds—Wes Walker, Verne Miller's Boys Club, tko'ed Jerry Cline, Liberal.
Heavyweight—John Ledesma, Wellington, dec. Bill Beck, Liberal.

CLASS B
112 pound—Tom Burns, WAC, over Tony Romanis, Wellington. (Referee awarded win to Burns judging it a no contest fight).
118 pounds—Harry Neal, Coffeyville, dec. Homer Hernandez, North End Athletic club.
126 pounds—Bob Eubanks, WAC, dec. Frank Morz, Vern Miller's Boys Club.
130 pounds—Gary Matson, WAC, dec. Clarence Ellis, Vern Miller's Boys Club.
135 pounds—Tom Lutkie, WAC, dec. Neil Edwards, Hutchinson.
147 pounds—Oscar Batts, Vern Miller's Boys Club, tko'ed Roger Norris, WAC.

SEMI-FINAL RESULTS
Class A
147 pound—Ivan Page, Hutchinson, dec. Turner Silman, Tulsa, Okla.
126 pound—Harold Wilson, Great Bend, TKO'ed Mike Webb, Ponca City, Okla.
Class B
160 pound—Tom Carlyle, Liberal, forfeit from Steve Boehm, Coffeyville.
112 pound—Tom Burns, WAC, KO'ed Ronny Morris, WAC.
126 pound—Bob Eubanks, WAC, TKO'ed Barney Roth, Great Bend.
147 pound—Frank Delgotta, Great Bend, forfeit over Dave Hearn, Vern Miller's BC.
135 pound—Neil Edwards, Hutchinson, dec. John Serriz, Wellington.
135 pound—Tom Lutkie, WAC, dec. Jim Reyes, Wellington.
147 pound—Wes Sullivan, Vern Miller's BC, TKO'ed A. J. Stone, Blackwell, Okla.
160 pound—Willard Woods, Vern Miller's BC KO'ed Hal McGuire, Blackwell, Okla.

February 17, 1962

By ...
Eagle Sports Editor

Ivan Page, Hutchinson, Kan., welterweight, and Wesley Walker, Wichita light heavyweight, scored impressive second and first round knockouts Friday night in the Wichita Forum as the Kansas Golden Gloves Boxing Tournament swung under way.

Page flattened Marion West, Wichita Athletic Club, 1 minute and 44 seconds of th second round. Page dumped th Wichitan with a sharp lef hoo. early in the round an then put him down for the fina count with a short barrage o hooks to the head.

Lands Big Punch

Walker, a member of Vern Miller's Boys' Club of Wichita, landed the biggest punch of the night in belting out Bobby Singleton, Ponca City, Okla., in the 175-pound bout division. The Wichita Negro connected with a leaping left hook to the chin of Singleton in a corner after 1 minute and 30 seconds of the first round.

The Ponca City fighter still was wobbly as he was helped from the ring.

Both were "open class" bouts.

Miller's Boys' Club also came up with a one-round knockout winner in the 126-pound novice class with Frank Morz stopping Albert Lewis, Coffeyville, Kan., in 1 minute and 16 second on a technical knockout. There were no knockdowns.

A crowd estimated at 2,500 fans, which included a balcony full of boy scouts, turned out for the opening night of the tourney.

Double-Winner

Jim Woods, Blackwell, Okla., was a double-winner on the card. The Oklahoma 147-pounder, using a good body attack, punched out a close decision over J. D. Others, Ponca City, Okla., in his first bout.

Woods then came back in the final bout on the program to cop a split decision over Jim Landis, a University of Oklahoma student fighting for the Wichita AC, to enter the "open" welterweight finals.

Several semifinals and 15 "open" and "novice" championship bouts are scheduled for the Forum Saturday night. The first of the semifinals will be in the ring at 7:30 o'clock.

The "open" champions will win berths on the Kansas team which will go to the National Golden Gloves Tournament in Chicago next week.

EVENT RESULTS
Class A (Open)
116 pounds—Carrol Eubank, Wichita AC, ko'd Howard Johnson, Great Bend, Kan., first round.
118 pounds—Henry Fullard, Coffeyville, Kan., decisioned Claude Harmon, Ponca City, Okla.
147 pounds—Jim Woods, Blackwell, Okla., won split-decision over J. D. Others, Ponca City, Okla.
160 pounds—Les Elbert, Blackwell, Okla., decisioned Arthur Blueback, Ponca City, Okla.
147 pounds—Jim Landis, Wichita AC, decisioned Tim Buffalohead, Newkirk, Okla.
175 pounds—Wesley Walker, Wichita Vern Millers Boys Club, knocked out Bobby Singleton, Ponca City, Okla., 1 min. and 30 sec. of first round.
147 pounds—Ivan Page, Hutchinson, Kan., knocked out Marion West, Wichita AC, 1 min., 44 sec., second round.

100

March 22, 1966

LAWRENCE BOXING CLUB—Manager Wesley Walker (far right) poses with six members of the Lawrence Boxing Club that won 10 of 13 fights in the recent Wichita Regionals. Because the winners were in the novice class, they were not eligible to compete in Kansas City's current national finals. Ex-boxer Walker needs crutches because he's still nursing an injury to his leg, suffered in a car accident about two years ago. In the picture, from left, assistant trainer Bob Nesman, Mark Brooks, Michael D. Murray, Tony Estelle, Stanley Graham, Leslie Steckel, Thomas D. DiBiase and Wesley. (Journal-World Photo)

2 Defending Champs Left In Golden Gloves Tourney

KANSAS CITY (AP) — The stubby little Miller brothers of Fairview, Mont., are the only defending champions left going into quarter-finals of the 39th National Golden Gloves Boxing Tournament tonight.

Two defending national champs from Detroit, middleweight Al Jones and light heavyweight Larry Charleston, were ousted in the second round Tuesday night.

Clay Hodges, heir-apparent to Jerry Quarry's heavyweight crown, helpd Los Angeles to the early lead in defense of its team title with an easy first round TKO.

Louisville's gifted Marcus Anderson, a two-time Gloves featherweight champion, is seeking the 135 crown this time. His quarter-final foe will be Tony Drake of Omaha, runner-up last year. Another top 135 fight matches Joe Epsinosa of Salt Lake City with Ronald Coleman of St. Louis.

Rolland Miller, a member of the Minneapolis team, takes on Roland Olivares of Fort Worth in a flyweight bout. Earl Large of Roswell, N.M., runner-up last year, faces Carl Evans of Indianapolis.

Mel Miller, the 118 champ, is a member of the Billings, Mont., team. A top threat to his crown is Cincinnati's John North, national AAU runner-up last year.

A crowd of 4,500 watched 66 bouts involving the four heaviest classes Tuesday night. The thing was clear — talent is overflowing in the 147 and 160-pound classes and above last year in 175 and heavyweight.

The welters include Hedgeman Lewis of Detroit, national AAU champ, and James Pars of Cleveland, 1965 Gloves runner-up who beat Lewis in the semifinals. Also, bald-headed Jim Neill of Buffalo, the welter champ of Ireland.

The middleweight class is tougher because of Salt Lake City's Joe Hopkins, runner-up to Charleston for the 175 crown last year, and William Douglas Jr., a 175 quarter-finalist last year. Douglas decked defending champ Jones three times with a hard right for a second round TKO.

Richard Steele of Los Angeles beat Charleston with a strong finish in their gruelling battle. Steel and the defending champ were even until then.

A pair of top heavyweight bouts tonight match Phillip Smith of Huntington with Edward Brooks of Milwaukee and Alvin Lewis of Detroit against James Howard of Buffalo.

Tonight's 32-bout card, all in one ring, will eliminate 32 men, leaving 32 for the semifinals and finals Friday — four in each of eight classes. Thursday is a day of rest.

Milwaukee was awarded the 1967 national tourney on Clarence Kenney's top bid. Cleveland's John Nagy was elected Gloves president.

Tom DiBiase Rates as Top Local Boxer; Others Cited

Novice heavyweight Tom J. DiBiase has been named outstanding boxer of the 1966 Lawrence Boxing Club, manager Wesley Walker has announced. DiBiase received a trophy during a banquet sponsored by the Lawrence Lions Club.

Other special trophies: Most courageous boxer, Stan Graham; sportsmanship, Harry Rayton Jr.; most conscientious trainer, Tony Estelle.

Receiving individual trophies at the banquet: novice featherweight, Joe Godfrey.

Open lightweight, Rudy Oberzan and Harry Rayton.

Open welterweight, Michael D. Murray.

Novice welterweight, Mark Brooks.

Novice middleweight, Hobart Woody, Tony Estelle.

Novice lightheavyweight, Leslie Steckel, Stan Graham.

Novice heavyweight, Tom J. DiBiase.

Not present for the presentation of the individual trophies: Novice lightweight Jim Fisher; novice welterweight Frank Lawson; novice lightheavyweight Rod Silverglat.

In the Wichita Golden Gloves Regionals this year, Walker's amateur boxers won 10 of 13 bouts in one of the finest local showings on record.

However, the champions were in the novice class, and novice fighters do not compete in the national finals, now in progress in Kansas City.

Clay Hodges, outstanding amateur heaveyweight from Los Angeles, was the featured speaker at the banquet.

Cassius Gets Bout License, But It's Non-Title Affair

TORONTO (AP) — Heavyweight champion Cassius Clay now has a license here for a 15-round bout against Canadian champion George Chuvalo March 29 that won't be recognized in Ontario as a title fight.

But if the 28-year-old Canadian strongboy ever gets lucky and hands the 24-year-old Louisville Lip his first defeat, you can bet that Chuvalo will be

valo winning are 7-1 at the moment. Still Clay was a 7-1 underdog the night he stopped Sonny Liston in seven at Miami Beach 25 months ago to win the title.

But if an undefeated, fast young, 6-foot-3, 210-pounder was 7-1 against Liston then some experts say Chuvalo should be at least 10-1 considering that his last effort was a losing one to Eduardo Corletti, the Argentine

Turner, McAfee Voted Into Hall

Lou Engel New Sports Editor, Replacing Morey

Lou Engel, a sports editor and writer in Colorado for the past six years, will become Journal-World sports editor effective April 5. Engel succeeds Earl Morey, who is to become director of public information for the Greater Kansas City Chamber of Commerce. Morey will edit "The Kansas Citian," a Chamber publication.

Engel, 33, is a native of Hebron, Neb., and comes to the Journal-World from the Pueblo, Colo., Chieftain. Before going to Pueblo in 1962, he was sports editor of the Colorado Springs Free Press, covering Air Force Academy activities.

A 1960 graduate of the Nebraska School of Journalism, Engel spent four years in the Air Force prior to entering college. As a student, he served as a reporter for the Alliance, Neb., Times-Herald and the Lincoln Star.

Engel and his wife have children, ages 5 and 7, and the family will move here as soon as school and housing arrangements can be made.

Morey, 40, joined the Journal-World staff in January of 1956 after working on the Pittsburg, Kan., Headlight-Sun and the Grand Island, Neb., Independent. During 1952, he worked as a line foreman at the Sunflower Ordnance Works.

He is a graduate of Pittsburg State College and he and his wife Pam have two children—Shari, a freshman at Kansas University, and Mike, a sophomore at Lawrence High. The family makes its home at 1739 Maple Lane, but plans to move to the Kansas City area in the near future.

A native of Frontenac, Kan., Morey is a World War II veteran of the Navy.

A's Ticket Push Is Thursday

KANSAS CITY (AP) — Thursday is Major League Baseball Day in Kansas City and a concentrated effort is planned to boost the season ticket sale for the Athletics.

Fifty teams of two men have been organized to call at busi-

Kansas Frosh Set Hot Pace In Loop Track

KANSAS CITY, Mo.—Few will deny that this was the best year in track history for Big Eight Conference freshmen. Times recorded for this year's Conference postal meet show that eight new records were set and two more tied. This was the strongest record-book onslaught since the meet originated.

As expected, the main mark mauler was Kansas' celebrated Jim Ryun, who came in with all-time freshman lows in the 880, 1,000, mile and two-mile to take the "record settingest" title away from another Kansan, Gene McClain, who had three last year. Ryun's performances paced Kansas to the team title. The Jayhawks had 79 3/10.

Right behind, and the real pusher on the track, was Kansas State. The Wildcats' Terry Davis stepped out to a new mark in the 440 and Mike Heer tied the 600 standard. It was in these two events the Manhattan entries scored over half their team points—13 in the 440 and 12 more in the 600. The Wildcats were second with 44¼.

Joining Ryun in the winners' circle and in the record book for Kansas were hurdler George Byers, who had a :06.7 for the 60 lows, high jumper Ken Gaines, who checked in with 6-9¾, and pole vaulter Bob Steinhoff, who tied for the title and record with 16-0¼.

Sharing the pole vault top with Steinhoff was Oklahoma's Larry Smith, who recorded his 16-0¼ in a head-to-heat battle with the Kansan at the Kansas State Invitational, winning over Steinhoff on fewer misses.

Oklahoma, the third-place team with 34 17/20, also owns a portion of the 60-dash record, thanks to the Longs, Glen and Wayne, both of whom had :06.1's in the 60 sprint this season. Oklahoma's Mike Gregory won the broad jump with 23-6¾ for the second Sooner bauble.

The only individual title not going to the Kansas teams or Oklahoma was the shot put, where Oklahoma State's Mike Ryles won with 53-7½.

Players Poli

Red

WINTER HAVEN, — The Boston Red S meeting in the early spring training. They doors on the mana coaches. It was for pla It lasted for two ho they called in Mana Herman and his coach

"They asked me to their plant to police, t on and off the field," man. "I agreed. I t very healthy situation

The Red Sox did housecleaning duri winter. They traded

McLain A For Long

By THE ASSOCIATE

Denny McLain was out away. Jim Bouton long way to go.

McLain, a hard-thro troit right-hander, wor innings — longest st pitcher this spring — gers mauled the New kees 7-4 Tuesday for t straight exhibition vict

Bouton, a troubled right-hander, worked nings and took his thir pounding. He yielded Detroit runs, including slam homer by Willi and bases-empty blast Demeter and Al Kaline

McLain, a week sho 22nd birthday, is com 16-6 season and his rosy. Bouton, 27, is fig a job after last year's lapse — and running morrows. Tuesday's rocketed his earned ru for the spring to 11.70.

Bobby Wine, Phila light-hitting shortstop, his first hit of the sprin inning homer that Phillies a 3-2 victory Los Angeles Dodgers.

California crushed 11-0; Atlanta edged Ka 4-3; Houston topped P 5-3; St. Louis defeate nati 6-4; Washingtor Boston 8-7; Baltimore New York Mets 5-3; th

SION CHAMPS. — Eight Golden Glove Champions, splay their hard earned trophies, which they were being the champion fighters in their division in the 1 Golden Gloves tournament. Front row (kneeling) t; Allen Lattimore, 112 pound division of Gateway; ple, 118 pound division, St. Benedict's; Walter Allen, 126 pound division, Pan-American; Thurnell Thompson, 135 pound division, Gateway; Standing, left to right; Jewell Shane, 147 pound division, Whatsoever club; Kenneth Maples, 160 pound division, Gateway; Wesley Walker, 175 pound division, Gateway and Frank House, heavyweight, Gateway.

ERNON SMITH, lef.. and WES WALKER will fight in the Golden Gloves Tournment of Champions in Kansas City this week for the Ottawa Boys Club. The open ss boxers live in Lawrence. Ean won a Golden Gloves jacket last week by ming ring foes in the finals of th preliminaries in Kansas City, Kas. Walker Smith were scheduled for bouts ast night but slick roads barred their way to nsas City.   (Herald Photo by Bob Leonard)

Walker Fight a Reality?

e the match possible.
ker, if he wants the fight,
t satisfy Carter's terms.
lker is ready and willing to

rpions Lead Boxers
ing Into Homestretch

RANKFURT—The CCA Scor-
is hold a slim three point
as Div boxers go into the
ie stretch of the 1959 season.
r - command bouts, Tuesday
Thursday, wind up action
il the Div championships,
ember 8 and 11.
tandings, exclusive of this
k's bouts, have CCA on top
h 63 points. CCB trails with

he late-coming CCC Cougars
I have an outside chance to
ch the leaders. They have 42
nts.
uesday night CCB hosts Div-
y and Thursday CCA visits
C.

lges Carter

other's domain. Walker finally
ided to reduce and make the
it possible.
'or Carter the defeat was the
rd heartache in two years and
first this season. A year ago
dropped two close decisions to
/ heavyweight champion Jim
inson.
Carter, pressing the attack with
fighting tactics, easily dominat-
the beleaguered Walker in the
st round. The DivArty boxer,
uld only counter with flurries
iich had little effect on the su-
rior-conditioned Carter.
Both fighters were dazed by the
id of round two after repeated
cchanges to the head—although
'alker seemed to hold a slight
lge.
The decisive canto was the third.
arter slammed Walker against
ie ropes in a near knockdown but
ie DivArty man reverberated
/ith right and left crosses in the
inal two minutes to carry the
ight decision.

meet Carter, but he isn't going to
lose weight to make the match
possible. Carter, if he wants the
fight, must satisfy Walker's terms.
So goes the Div boxing merry-
go-round.

Both Own Good Records

Carter is CCB's classy light
heavyweight who nearly stopped
giant Jim Johnson as a heavyweight last year. Walker is Div-
Arty's power-punching heavyweight who scrapped as a light
heavyweight a year ago and then
lost his only Army bout in the
USAREUR championships as a
middleweight.
Neither of the fighters have formidable foes in their respective
weight brackets this year.

Dream Match

Div fight fans couldn't ask for a
better pairing than a Walker-
Carter bout, but it's a dangerous
proposition for the fighters if
they're aiming for clean slates.
Someone is bound to lose and with
the loss may go dreams of a Div
crown.
Will fight fans ever see the
dream match between Carter and
Walker?
That's up to Carter and Walker.
They have two more opportunities to compromise on their original stands: 1) next Thursday,
when CCB and DivArty pugilists
go after each other at Coleman
Kaserne; and, 2) at the Div boxing championships in December.

Wes Walker
... isn't losing weight

CCB-DivArty Tie Matches At Coleman

GELNHAUSEN — The
Warriors of DivArty met the
Braves of CCB at Coleman
Kaserne last week, and slugged
away to an 11-11 standoff.
Leon Noel chalked up his fourth
straight knockout by jolting Div-
Arty's Gary Spears in :32 seconds
of the first round. It marked the
redhead's second straight first
round knockout.
In a welterweight clash, Tom
Wachs overcame some effective
counterpunching by DivArty's John
Jones and stopped the Spearheader
in 1:35 of the last round. Wachs
pinned Jones to the ropes in the
finale and was pounding Jones at
will before the referee intervened.
CCB's Gary Ammons won by a
technical knockout over DivArty
slugger Aaron Hickman in 1:38 of
third round. Ammons, smarting
from a recent KO defeat, stalked
Hickman for two rounds before the
fight was stopped by a knee injury
sustained by Hickman.
In the slowest bout of the evening, DivArty's Willie Crockett decisioned CCB's Orville Wright.
Crockett came on after losing the
first round to outpoint Wright.
In the opening bout, speedy
Roosevelt Smith outclassed hard
boxing Bob Lavene in a welter-go.
CCB's Lavene, looking for a one-
punch KO, never found the mark.
An adept left by Smith earned a
close decision.
Dave Jones, CCB featherweight,
and DivArty's flyweight Jim V
liams, both won by forfeit.

THE JAB—Orville Wright, a non-flying heavyweight from CCB, shoved home a right jab into the bread
basket of DivArty's Willie Crockett in bouts at Coleman Kaserne. Crockett won the decision, but the team
totals tied, 11-11.
—HARTMAN

Middleweight Robinson Gets Chance

Floors Victim In First Real Boxing Match

John Robinson
. . . wasn't surprised about the knockout
—Young

GELNHAUSEN—John, Robinson CCB middleweight, knocked out CCA's John Sullivan in 30 seconds of the first round last week. The impressive KO serves warning to competing commands that CCB has a formidable middleweight entrant for the Division championships.

Robinson entered the Kirch-Goens match virtually untested—yet he owned a record of four wins and no defeats. His previous victories came on forfeits and disqualifications.

The win against Sullivan, however, gives him considerable stature in local fight circles.

Robinson wasn't surprised about the knockout. "Coach (Jim) Moore concentrated on improving my punching power," he said.

He also taught Robinson to hit in combinations. "In this fight I remembered what Moore taught me . . . and it worked," the boxer said. A left to the body and a right to the head were his payoff punches.

This is the 48th Inf soldier's second year in the ring.

Before entering the Army Robinson was a professional singer in New York City. Primarily a rhythm and Blues singer, he was vocalizing in several Manhattan clubs when the Korean conflict broke out.

Right now he sings for the Johnny Largo Combo, a popular Gelnhausen group. On several occasions Robinson has had the unusual experience of performing in the ring on Friday night and entertaining on Saturday.

A keen observer of boxers himself, Robinson listed the men in the Division which he considers the best.

He selected CCB heavyweight Willie Carter; Div Trns light heavy Wes Walker; CCB middleweight Leon Noel; CCB light middleweight John Mayfield; CC light-welterweight Arnold Jack CCA lightweight Willie Little and CCB featherweight Don Riley.

He modestly omitted the name of John Robinson from the li

James Moore

OUR CCB BOXERS AND TRIOS
Div Trns and CCA forged sion ring titles while two irheaders advanced to USAR-t crowns. It all added up to a derfully successful year for the boxing program and Jim re, CCB and Division coach.

ack in February we quoted re as saying, "This is the best ing team we've had since the Armd Division arrived in ope." This statement proved to accurate, for not only did the ad fashion a pair of champs—lso gripped third place among nine commands represented at AREUR.

lthough the two titlists didn't l from Moore's home command, B, he was instrumental in push-them to USAREUR championps. It was his decision to enter h Willie Littles and Bill White weight brackets other than the s they were accustomed to. is turned the tide. The result s a "first" for the Division: Never before had the 3d Armd Division imed a pair of USAREUR boxing champs. Obviously, the boxing coach of the year is Jim Moore. And, just as vious, the top fighters of the year are Willie Littles and Bill White.

Pfc Saves German Boy in Main

Pfc Donald Lanouette
. . . rescues youth

HANAU — A five-year-old German boy was rescued from the icy waters of the Main River here Nov. 20 by Pfc Donald Lanouette of Co E, 23d Eng Bn.

Lanouette was doing a periodic maintenance check on one of the 27-foot boats his company uses for bridge construction when excited cries from children on the bank drew his attention to a small figure bobbing up and down out in the river.

The 19-year-old power boat operator dove in and swam 30 feet to the spot where young Stani Klimcik was on the point of sinking below the surface for the second time. Clasping Stani under one arm, Lanouette made for the shore, where the boy was wrapped in a field jacket and taken to his home nearby.

Expert Swimmer

Apparently the boy was playing on the river bank near the Gross Auheim barge area when he fell in and was swept downstream by the currents of the Main. Tucked away in his bed after doses of hot tea and cognac, Stani was shaken but otherwise unharmed by the experience.

Stani's mother, who works at the Teenage (1319) Club here, expressed her gratitude to the soldier who had saved her son's life.

Lanouette, an expert swimmer, was a member of his high school swimming team in New Haven, Conn.

CCC Boxers Bow to Division Trains, 12-1

HANAU—A strong but numerically impotent CCC box-squad put up a vigorous front in efforts to defend 1957 3d Armd Division championship here last week re falling to rival Div Tns, 12-11.

Friedberg's CCC representatives captured four of the ning's bouts, but forfeitures in the bantam, light and htheavy weight classes earned Tns six gift points.

The turning point came when Div Tns middleweight ocked out the Cougars' Gibson in one minof the second round.

Takes Eight Count

ly offensive to stun Gibson, but the and for a moment Gibson turned t down for the compulsory eight another speed attack to close out

In the meantime Friedberg's Lonnie Johnson (welterweight), Hubie Lavender (light welterweight), Dan Pinkney (welterweight) and John Mayfield (light middleweight) registered decisions over Hanau's Harry Davis, Roosevelt Smith, George Hudson and Leon Wilbon.

Takes Close Decision

In heavyweight action CCC's Jim King won over Al Thames in a hair-splitting decision. Thames used a controlled attack against King's unorthodox stance.

Failure of Friedberg's squad to meet weigh-in requirements in all brackets gave automatic wins to Div Tns bantamweight Jim Williams, lightweight John Jones and light heavyweight Wes Walker.

Both fighters failed to produce any action in a heavy-weight exhibition match between CCC's Wally Foster and Tns' Will Crockett. The referee halted the fight and

BANTAMWEIGHT—Jim Williams (Tns) won (no opponent).
FEATHERWEIGHT—Chuck Robinson (CCC forfeit (no opponent).
WELTERWEIGHT—Lonnie Johnson (CCC Harry Davis, Jr. (Tns).
LIGHTWEIGHT—John Jones (Tns) won on opponent).
LIGHT WELTERWEIGHT—Hubie Lavender cisioned Roosevelt Smith (Tns).
WELTERWEIGHT—Dan Pinkney (CCC) George Hudson (Tns).
LIGHT MIDDLEWEIGHT—John Mayfield (C sioned Leon Wilbon (Tns).
MIDDLEWEIGHT—Dick Manzy (Tns) KOd R son (CCC).
LIGHT HEAVYWEIGHT—Wes Walker (Tns) forfeit (no opponent).
HEAVYWEIGHT—Jim King (CCC) decisioned Al T

A WILD LEFT misses Bill Crockett (right), Division Trains heavyweight hopeful, in a sparring match with teammate Wes Walker (left). Both men expect to see action in tonight's opener for Division Trains. —Snope

KO Specialis
Walker Goes
After His Man

HANAU — Wes Walker, Division Trains light-heavyweight, has spent only a little over two minutes in Army rings—but those minutes have provided fight fans with some of the most electrifying action seen in Division bouts this year.

Walker, a solid 178 pounds standing 5-10, has scored two consecutive knockouts and both were in the first round.

Against CCB's Hal Malone, Walker won in 1:19 and brought the KO time down to :55 against CCA's Bill Bettis.

The 23-year-old fighter from the 23d Engr Bn has a lifetime record of 26 wins and three losses.

Walker's successes in his pre-Army fight career include the Topeka (Kansas) Golden Gloves novice championship in 1955 and the Kansas City Golden Gloves open championship for three straight years from 1956 to 1958.

When Walker comes into the ring he knows the advantage of rapid offensive.

Fans who have seen him in action wonder what it would be like if the fight were to go longer than the customary first round. Walker is aware of this and so he tries to pace himself. "But the opportunity resents itself," says Walker, "I won't let it go. So far the opportunities have been enormous.

Jim Johnson, Locomotives coach has high hopes for his most dramatic fighter. "Without looking too far ahead," says Johnson, "I

Ring Favorites . . .

Braves Command Advantage
At Start of Stretch Drive

FRANKFURT — Three more weeks may tell the tale. If CCB boxers can maintain the torrid point pace established during the first half of the 3d Armd Division command-level boxing program, the Braves will enter the February championship matches as heavy favorites.

Today, with three big team pairings still on the schedule for each command squad, CCB has earned 46 points — 15 more than runner-up CCA. Div Trns and CCC trail by 16.

CCB is pinning hopes on reliable heavyweight Willie Carter, welterweight Tom Wachs and featherweight Don Ridley. Carter has three knockouts to his credit in as many fights.

Lightweight Willie Littles and middleweight Vince Pinto were the only men that showed

a winning spark in CCA's most recent outing.

Jim Johnson, last year's Division heavyweight champ from Div Trns, has decided to come out of self-imposed retirement. Hanau boxing fans figure he may be the important spark which could ignite a potentially strong Trns outfit. The fight of the year may pit Johnson and CCB's undefeated Carter at Hanau, Jan 16.

At Friedberg light-welterweight Arnold Jack and featherweight Chuck Robinson have been the bulwarks.

Johnson

Overtime Comments

by Wednesday, April 8, 1959

TO SELECT THE MOST OUTSTANDING ATHLETE in the Division during the past year is next to impossible. It's like picking the Man of the Year on the planet Earth. There are many men with far reaching significance and profound effect on the year's events, In a reduced way this is true when applied to 3d Armd Division sports.

All of us can, and probably do, have our personal opinions and prejudices on the selection of a top athlete. What denominators do we use to weight an individual's ability and dedication to his athletic endeavors? Then, is this the desired or correct approach to use?

There are perhaps 20 athletes that can be nominated as the best in the Division. It might be easier to do this than to single out one man.

But like everyone else we have our opinions and prejudices. Admittingly this may not be an accurate choice and many may disagree, but Jim Johnson leads the list in our book. He is the 3d Armd Division's best athlete.

Johnson's appearance on the scene ever since he arrived in Europe as a member of the 57th AAA Bn has been frequent and always consistent in high standards of sportsmanship and achievement. A two

Jim Johnson

sports man, Johnson excels as a boxer and as a football player. After the 1958 season with the Hanau Locomotives the hard-hitting fullback was selected by his teammates as the Most Valuable Player on the grid team.

The esteem his opponents hold for him was evident in The Spearhead Newspaper all-star poll, Johnson received more votes than any other player, and this includes some of USAREUR's best.

It was a delight to watch the Div Trns hulwark perform on the football field during the past season. His tremendous power often made tacklers wish they had never made the attempt to ground his 225-pound frame.

Unfortunately Johnson has not always performed with a well-balanced team. He has seen his share of losses, but has always guided his teammates to a respectable showing.

It was heart-breaking to see Johnson lose out in his USAREUR heavyweight title fight last month after building up a lead in the early rounds. But anyone who saw the

Walker

think Walker should take the Division championship."

Johnson feels assured that Walker is in top-flight condition and that he could go the full distance if necessary.

Walker played some basketball and football in high school, but these sports didn't leave him with the feeling of satisfaction and accomplishment that he has when he leaves the ring.

"There," he says, "it's my

Div Boxers Survive Regional, Enter USAREUR Fracas

FRANKFURT—More than half of the Spearhead boxing delegation to the Northern Regional Boxing slate of USAREUR came unscathed through ring action at Kaiserslautern and will do battle in the USAREUR quarterfinals in Hanau this weekend.

Five Division fighters won their way to the quarterfinals the hard way and four more made the trip by way of byes and defaults. Sixteen fighters traveled to Kaiserslautern from Gelnhausen—training headquarters—for the bouts.

Pounding their way to victory were Jim Johnson, Div Trns, Wes Walker, Div Trns, Willie Carter, CCB, Elmo Brooks, CCB, and William White. Johnson was the only knockout victor of the group.

Wes Walker Wins

Fighting for the first time in the middleweight class, knockout specialist Wes Walker went three rounds to defeat Vernon Garrett, Area Comds. Walker, winning a unanimous decision, gained the nod on aggressiveness and counter-punching.

Walker had Garrett in trouble twice, and carried most of the rounds, but the fight was more even than the final scoring indicated.

Willie Carter, in the lightheavyweight slot, banked on sharp punching to easily out-point Joseph Martin, V Corps. Although the Spearhead slugger failed to knock down his opponent, Carter was fast and accurate in gaining the decision.

Elmo Brooks, darkhorse of the lightmiddle class, fired a steady barrage of punches throughout three rounds to gain a close decision over Tommy Byrd of V Corps.

Biding his time—and precious little of it at that—Div heavyweight Jim Johnson stalked D. C. Hale of the 8th Div before cornering and unleashing dynamite-laden punches that put Hale out of comprehension in 1:45 of the first round.

William White, Division lightweight, easily outclassed Edward Ludy, Area Comds, by employing a stiff left and using a short right uppercut to upset his opponent. White early gained the edge of advantage over Ludy, and kept up his superior pace until the end of the bout.

Wach's Streak Ends

Tom Wachs fight win streak came to a shuddering halt after a close welterweight decision in favor of his opponent, Don Stewart of the 8th Inf Div. Wachs was effective from the inside, but he kept running into stiff jabs of Stewart—enough, apparently, to come out on the short end of the decision.

In a lightweight clash, Jack Ableman, V Corps, decisioned Dave Jones in a toe-to-toe battle. Ableman, veteran of 83 fights, won on a steady body attack that wilted Jones. The fight was close, though Jones was evidently tired at the end.

Another welterweight go saw Aaron Hickman of Div Trns, drop a decision to Jim Williams of V Corps. Williams out-jabbed and out-lasted the unorthodox slugger Hickman. The decision was a close one, with William's better boxing talents responsible for the winning edge.

John Finch of Area Comd defeated fleet-footed Clarence Pinkney in a light welter encounter. After two fast rounds, Pinkney tired in the final and crucial canto under steady body punching from the heavier Finch.

Southpaw Edward Amerantes, Area Comd flyweight, caught Spearhead's James Williams with a felling left hook and went on to press his advantage and win the bout.

Leon Noel won his way to Hanau on a default. Going into USAREUR on byes are Willie Littles, featherweight, Al Thames, heavyweight, and John R hinson, middleweight.

USAREUR QUARTERFINALS

JOHNSON • CARTER •
NOEL • WHITE BROOKS
LITTLES • WALKER •
ROBINSON • THAMES

Spearhead REPRESENTATIVES

THURS FRI SAT 8 PM

FLIEGERHORST GYM • HANA

Featherweight champ Cal Huddleston just misses a right intended

Dec. 1957

Things are pretty grim for flyweights Jose Mojica (left) and Jim Williams — at least their facial expressions indicate such. Williams

Crook-Walker Bout Headlines Boxing Card at Sports Center

by Bill Fidati

More than 3,000 boxing fans are expected to jam the Sports Center Hall tomorrow night to see Berlin Command's top pugilists, spearheaded by fiery Eddie Crook, trade punches with a tough 3rd Armored Division team. The fights are slated to start at 7 p.m.

Fighters on the 3rd Armored Division squad are drawn from four combat commands in the Frankfurt area. Standouts among them are middleweight Wesley Walker, a former Golden Glover from Kansas City who reached the USAREUR semi-finals last year, and USAREUR lightweight champ Bill White.

Although Walker is no stranger to the ring wars, he will probably be tackling the toughest opponent of his career tomorrow night when he climbs through the ropes to challenge Crook, All-Army, USAREUR and CISM light-middleweight titleholder.

Walker has compiled a 31-5 record since he started boxing as an amateur in 1955. Besides being a Golden Gloves middleweight champ, the accomplished southpaw has reigned as 3rd Armored Division lightheavyweight king and has also campaigned as a heavyweight.

Weight Advantage

He will weigh in approximately eight pounds heavier and stand four inches taller than Crook for tomorrow's bout. Crook, who claims his best fighting weight is 154, hopes to carry 156 pounds into the ring with him.

Despite Walker's height, weight and reach advantages and his impressive record, most local prognosticators are putting their chips on Crook, a wizened ring warrior who has lost only eight times in more than 200 Army bouts.

"Eddie will take him," smiled Bill Sherry, an ex-boxer who constitutes one-half of the BC coaching staff. "But I'm too superstitious to predict knockout."

Sandy Sandlin, the other half of the BC braintrust, isn't quite as cautious. "I saw Walker fight last year and think Eddie, who is one of the best amateurs I've ever seen in my 11 years with service boxing, should get him in the second round."

Crook by KO

Even more outspoken on the subject is Jim Asente, BC sports chief, who openly predicted that "Crook will put his man away whenever he sees fit in the second or third round, providing Walker is a good fighter. If Walker has a bad night, Crook will knock him out in the first round to prevent himself from looking bad."

And the man with whom no has gone the distance in the two years, Eddie Crook! He mod said, "I'll be in there to win. I to land sharp punches and if ker's ever in trouble, I'll try to him away. But I mainly want to w so if the fight goes the distance an I take a decision, that's fine too. I've seen Walker fight twice and know he's a good strong boy."

Crook claims the he's in excellent shape and hitting harder with both hands than at this time last year. Even though Walker is a lefthander, Crook doesn't think he'll have to alter his own cautious style of fighting.

Other top BC fighters who are scheduled to see action are Bill Magouirk, Herb Nelson, Fernie Estrada, Phil Yuen, Al Thompson and Barney Harrell.

Crooks Stops Walker in First To Pace Berlin Over 3d Armd

BERLIN (Special) — All Army and interservice middleweight king Eddie Crook bombed his way to an easy one-round knockout of Wesley Walker Saturday night.

Crook, pacing Berlin Comd boxers to victory over 3d Armd Div fighters, threw only a half-dozen punches at Walker who backpedaled throughout the one minute and 38 seconds he survived.

With less than a minute gone, Crook dropped Walker with a sharp left hook. Walker staggered to his feet at the count of eight, but was back on his pants for good a little later when Crook cut loose with an even more devastating left.

The referee stopped the fight with Walker sprawled on the ring apron.

Crook's win climaxed the eight-bout card, and enabled Berlin Comd to win the meet, five bouts to three.

Welterweight Fernie Estrada, Berlin, kept a capacity crowd of 3,500 at the Sports Center Hall cheering for three furious rounds as he decisioned Tom Wachs.

Both fighters were covered with Wachs' blood, which began pouring from his nose in the first round.

In a rousing lightweight bout Bill White, 3d Armd Div, had to settle for a decision over Bill Magorirk, even though he knocked Magorirk to the canvas in the first and second rounds. White won the USAREUR lightweight title in 1959.

The results:

BANTAMWEIGHT—Bill Nelson, 3d Armd Div, decisioned Bill Yuen.
LIGHTWEIGHT—Don Ridley, 3d Armd Div, decisioned Alonzo Carter; Bill White, 3d Armd Div, decisioned Bill Magorirk.
LIGHT-WELTERWEIGHT — Al Thompson, Berlin, decisioned Dan Pinkney.
WELTERWEIGHT — Fernie Estrada, Berlin Comd, decisioned Tom Wachs.
MIDDLEWEIGHT—Herb Nelson, Berlin Comd, decisioned Cliff Young; Barney Harrell, Berlin Comd, KOd Milt Boiano, 1:25 (1st); Eddie Crook, Berlin Comd, KOd Wesley Walter, 1:38 (1st).

Walker Go Saturday Fight of Berlin Card

LL, Staff Writer

nobody wants to Eddie Crook, will have month at the Sports when he meets Wesley

the USAREUR semiwon the Topeka, Kan., leweight title. Walker Golden Gloves middleyears.

and five losses. Since lost only two fights, hn Fuller, the 8th Div was Fuller who eliminsemifinals.

According to Jim Moore, coach of the 3d Armd Div team, Walker is more of a boxer than a slugger.

"I saw the last fight Crook lost and I know his weak points," Moore explained. "I feel if Wes fights him the same way he'll take Crook."

Back in Berlin, Crook said he was happy to get into the ring again after a long layoff. He needs bouts badly to tune up for the 1960 Olympic tryouts.

"Walker's tough and I'm giving him eight pounds," he said. "But I'd rather wear out than rust out."

Another big battle of the evening is expected to develop between Berlin's Bill Magouirk and the 3d Armd Div's Bill White, the 1958 USAREUR lightweight champion.

Berlin's Phil Yuen (left) tries to sneak in to nail the 3d Armd Div's Bill Nelson, but the Spearheader gained the better of this exchange. Nelson, a bantamweight, decisioned Yuen to win one of three bouts captured by the 3d Armd Div. (Army photo)

Berlin Takes 3d Armd Div In Exhibition Fight Card

BERLIN—Ed Crook threw only four or five punches, but that was all he needed to retire middleweight Wes Walker at 1:38 of the first round as Berlin Command boxers won five of eight exhibition fights from the 3d Armd Div last Saturday.

Crook, who holds numerous titles ranging from USAREUR to All-Army and CISM, floored Walker for an eight-count and then sent him down for good. This marks the first time in a 40-fight career that Walker has been retired.

Walker's only consolation was the fact that he's only the second Army boxer to challenge Crook this season. The other was the 8th Inf's Ed Kitchen who quit in the second round.

The 3d Armd Div captured the first three fights as bantamweight Bill Nelson, featherweight Don Ridley and lightweight Bill White all earned decisions, but Berlin came back to take the match with five straight victories.

Berlin's victors were welterweight Al Thompson, middleweight Herb Nelson, middleweight Barney Harrell, light middleweight Fernando Estrada and Crook.

The most unusual fight pitted featherweight Ridley against novice welterweight Alonzo Carter. Carter outweighed his opponent by 20 pounds, but the more experienced Ridley carried the fight all the way and earned an easy decision.

The night's shortest fight was Harrell's bout with the 3d Armd Div's Milt Boiano. Harrell delivered an uppercut that stopped the fray at 1:25 of the first round.

s Crook The Spook Of Boxing?

By Vince Mullahy

THE photo on the right on this page was taken by one Chris Connell of the Berlin Command PIO office.

As far as we're concerned, it's a classic of its kind.

It tells far better than the proverbial 10,000 words just why guys over the command ring field just don't want to get in the ring with Berlin's Eddie Crook.

In the photo, that's Crook over in the left corner, figuratively picking his teeth, 59 seconds after the "bout" began. The legs, sticking out from the midst of a group of solicitous handlers, belong to Wesley Walker, of the 3d Armd Div, who, 59 seconds before became one of those rare individuals who did have the guts to step into the ring with Crook.

So, this photo tells the old story. Kayo by Crook.

Besides being the big mainstay for a whirlwind Berlin Bears football team over the past couple of years, Crook has belted his way though the light-middleweight ranks to earn for himself Usareur, All-Army and Inter-Service titles—and all via the fast-knockout route.

He's no youngster, either. He's currently somewhere around the neighborhood of 30, but he's got his eyeballs glued to the Olympics in Rome later this year.

However, also at his age, he has no illusions about going any further. All he wants to do is take an Olympic crown. He realizes that the pro ranks are not for those edging the thirties, but he also realizes that anyone riding on a record such as his has a good chance of copping one of those gold medals in Rome.

That's his ambition. We think he's got what it takes to grab it.

We sure hope so, at any rate.

AND, while we seem to be stuck in the strands of the local boxing business, let's just wave a wild one for the guys who put on that V Corps Championship last week over at Pioneer Casern in Hanau.

It was a fine windup to the Corps program with, perhaps, the biggest disappointment to the overflow crowd coming in the light-heavyweight final when Charlie Scruggs did a walk-on to take the title without raising his hands.

(Continued on Page 17)

SPEAKING OF SPORTS
Strictly Personal

AAU Ring To

by EARL MOREY

WESLEY WALKER OF LAWRENCE continues to amaze me. He's retired two or three times from the amateur boxing ranks in order to coach and train younger fighters. But it seems something always comes up that causes Wes to crawl back into the ring, and each time he does, he enjoys success.

After Walker won the Kansas City Golden Gloves light heavyweight title, he "hung up the gloves." But he returned later to challenge Kansas University's Ron Marsh in the finals of the heavyweight division last year, and forced much younger Ron to the limit before losing a close decision.

Again, Walker quit as an active fighter and went to work building a team for the Lawrence Boxing Club, under the sponsorship of the Lions Club. But when he recently took a pair of fighters to Springfield, Mo., for matches, it was Wesley who had to take on one of Joplin's top heavies because another fighter failed to show. Wesley whipped the man easily.

Now he's won the Regional AAU heavyweight title and is in Las Vegas, Nev., trying for a berth in the Olympic trials which follow in New York. And you know something? Wes just might get the job done at both places. Don't bet against this battler.

⋆ ⋆ ⋆

Heads Into I

2 SoNev I
Semi-fina

B

Champions will
a team that will rep
ion in next month'
selected tonight as
Boxing Championsh
vention Center.

The semi-final
will start at 8 p.m.

Talent ranges
pound heavyweight
the tiny 112-pound
Jeans, who fights ir
title defender still ir

Two Southern Neva
ciation entrants wer
the semi-finalist:
Skip) Houk in the
division and Jim Eva
light-heavyweight cla
and Evans, both of I
intercollegiate cham
year while competir
University of Neva
team.

The 40 boxers in
finals are survivors
inal field of 168 whicl
from all corners of
States and as far aw
to Rico, Canada and

Mathis, the bigge
sibly the most jo
weight in AAU hist
hit of the quarter-f
day. He gained fi
outpointing Wes
Lawrence, Kan., a
the crowd in the

He peppered his
ponent with autho
as light on his fe
dancer. When Wal
age to get through
with left-right co
drew a broad smil
is.

The humble, 19-
a sign painter by
an expert roller
accounts for his

WEEK OF JANUARY 28
PAGE 2
to FEBRUARY 3, 1966
THE CALL, K. C., Mo.

LAWRENCE, Kas.—Ninth Street Baptist church, 847 Ohio, Rev. John V. Harris, pastor: Sunday school convened at 9:30 a.m. with morning worship following at 11 o'clock. The pastor's morning sermon topic was "The Law and the Gospel." The pastor's evening topic was "The Greatest Sentence Ever Written."

St. Luke A.M.E. church, 900 New York St., Rev. E. Lewis Branch, minister: Sunday school met at 9:45 a.m. with classes for all ages. The Senior choir processional was at 11 a.m., Miss Frances Bradley, organist, and Mrs. Helen Logan, pianist. Mrs. Eva Fishback was soloist, singing "Ask What You Will." The sermon by the pastor was entitled "A Spiritual Fog."

Wesley Walker and Jesse Milan were visitors, accompanied by the boys of the St. Luke basketball team which they coach. A—

METRO LEAGUE KINGS—The Slow Breaks went undefeated this season, and captured the Metro League basketball title in City Recreation Commission-sponsored play at the Community Building. The squad, front from left, Willis Brooks, Larry Hatfield and Will Mumford. Back row from left, Wesley Walker, John Hadl, Francis Ludvicek and Tom Boyd. (Journal-World Photo).

16-Year-Old Captures 147-Lb. Championship

By RON AMOS
R-J Sports Editor

Jessie Valdez, a 16-year-old Junior high school student from Houston, Tex., is the sensation of the Amateur Athletic Union boxing world today.

Valdez battled his way to the 147-pound championship in the 1964 National AAU Senior Boxing Championships Friday night at Convention Center and was honored even further by being named the tournament's outstanding fighter.

The youthful fighter won an upset decision over intercollegiate champion Martin (Skip) Houk of Reno in the afternoon semi-finals, and came back to score an even bigger upset in the final round over Quincy Daniels of the Air Force, a bronze medal winner in the 1960 Olympic Games in Rome.

All of it was quite a feat for a boy making his first appearance in a national tournament. Despite his youth, Valdez is quite a veteran. He's been boxing since he was 11 years old and showed it in the way he handled his two more experienced opponents.

In both cases, it was a matter of more speed and boxing skill.

The team title in the three-day event went to the Michigan association, headquartered in Detroit, with 10 points.

Champions were crowned in nine other divisions Friday night.

Buster Mathis, the laughing giant from Grand Rapids, Mich., who delighted the sparse crowds throughout the tournament with his agility and sense of humor in the ring, overpowered Al Wilson of the Marines in the finale.

Mathis, a six-foot-three 293-pound sign painter, literally flopped on the floor when he heard the decision.

Other winners were:

Bob Christopherson of the Air Force nailed the 178-pound title by outpointing Rudy Brown of Washington D.C.

— Will Cross of Portland TKO'd Robert McMillian of Toledo to capture the 165-pound crown. McMillian won the Golden Gloves title in that division.

— Hard-hitting Toby Gibson of Spokane cut up Pete Esquibel of Clovis, N. M., in the 156-pound final, winning a second-round TKO.

— Freddie Ward of Portland decisioned Tom Davis of Salt Lake City to annex 139-pound laurels.

— In the 132-pound class, Ron Harris of Detroit outpointed Herb Dallison of Washington D. C.

— Charles Brown of the Marines won a second-round TKO over Pete Spanakos of New York City for the 125-pound title when Spanakos suffered a cut over his right eye.

— Art Jones of San Francisco decisioned Gerry Lot of New Orleans, the defending champion, in the 119-pound division.

— A pair of 16-year-old Melvin Miller of Butte, Mont and Wallace Brooks of Phoenix met in the 112-pound finals with Miller winning a decision.

A special Nevada Centennial Commission sportsmanship award went to Gibson.

The 10 winners will represent the AAU in the Final Olympic Tryouts May 18-20 at Flushing N.Y. The team will train at Bolling Air Force Base at Washington, D.C.

Besides the AAU, the tryouts will draw 10 champions each from the Army, Navy, Air Force, Marines, Golden Gloves and the western and eastern regional tournaments.

THE GIANT — Buster Mathis, left, 293-pound heavyweight fr pids, Mich., laughingly backs away from "charging" Jim Hal afternoon's semi-finals of the 1964 National AAU Senior Box ships at Convention Center. Mathis decked Hall twice in route decision. R-J PHOTO BY

FINALS

112 pounds—Melvin Miller, Butte, Mont., outpointed Wallace Brooks, Phoenix, Ariz.
119 pounds—Art Jones, Air Force, outpointed Gerry Lott, New Orleans.
125 pounds — Charles Brown, Marines, stopped Pete Spanakos, New York 1:12.1.
132 pounds—Ron Harris, Detroit, outpointed Herb Dallason, Washington, D.C.
139 pounds—Freddie Ward, Seattle, outpointed Tom Davis, Salt Lake City.
147 pounds—Jessie Valdez, Houston, outpointed Quincy Daniels, Air Force.
156 pounds — Toby Gibson, Spokane, Wash., stopped Pete Esquibel, Clovis, N.M., 2.
165 pounds — Will Cross, Portland, stopped Robert McMillian, 1:44.2.
178 pounds—Bob Christopherson, Air Force, outpointed Rudy Brown, Washington, D.C.
Heavyweights — Buster Mathis, Grand Rapids, Mich., outpointed Al Wilson, Ma

REVIEW-JOURNAL

Sports

Las Vegas Review-Journal 13
Saturday, April 11, 1964

mifinals, Finals Slated
Golden Gloves Tonight

VALKENBURG
ss Sports Writer

TY (AP) — Top
bouts tonight in
he 39th National
Boxing Champi-
bald-headed Jim
falo, N.Y., vs.
is of Detroit and
Anderson of
., vs. shuffling
ght of Los An-

e two in excite-
be heavyweight

★ ★ ★

GES, the battling young amateur heavyweight
and close friend of Lawrence's Wesley Walker.
impression on members of the Lawrence Lions
evening.

evening was spent paying tribute to members
Boxing Club and manager Walker. Hodges, as
ey, was the featured speaker.

ar student at Southern Cal, Hodges, who plans
attorney, not only is big and impressive looking,
articulate.

dit to amateur boxing," County Attorney Ralph
er of the Lions, said.

ted out that despite the size of Los Angeles,
rs get a better shake out of life, thanks to
ley and the Lions.

★ ★ ★

HAT in the Los Angeles area, the youngsters
e gyms where the pros train. There are no
for the amateurs.

went on, after a youngster has had a few fights
good, he's invited to turn pro before he's
fully develop.

lodges said. "It's already happened to me."
like Hodges and Walker in the game, amateur
ood hands.

nore and more groups get behind the local
ake it a whopping success. The program de-
upport.

Clay Hodges of Los Angeles vs. big Earl Averette of Cleveland and hard-hitting light heavy John Griffin of Cleveland vs. Earl Howard of Kansas City.

Semifinals and finals will be packed into the last night, starting at 7 p.m., CST. Gloves officials hope for a near-sellout in 10,000-seat Municipal Auditorium, although the first three nights drew 13,000.

The Neill-Lewis bout might produce the 147 champ, although the winner may have to contend with James Parks of Cleveland. talented southpaw who was runner-up in 1965 and a former Eastern Olympic semi-finalist.

Neill, 23, hits hard but maintains a gay mood throughout each bout. The stringbean left-hander is welter champ of Ireland and a fine boxer. A wig is lifted from his head the moment the bell rings. Lewis was the AAU welter champ in 1965 and gloves 135 champ in 1964.

Fullbright stalks his foe slowly and with a cock-sure scowl, left arm dangling and explosive right hand cocked. He is hard to hit but the talented Anderson, two-time 126 champ, is good enough to score heavily.

Anderson, 19, is coached by Joe Martin, Cassius Clay's ex-trainer.

The 24-year-old Hodges pacing the Los Angeles bid for another team title, wears horned rimmed glasses when not in the ring and some call him a poor man's Clark Kent (Superman). He's 6-4, 206 pounds and handsome.

Brothers Rolland (Boom Boom) Miller, 20, the flyweight champ, and Mel Miller, 18, bantam champion will go after two more crowns. Both are from Fairview, Mont. Rolland, competing for Minneapolis, will meet Frank Vigil, Salt Lake City. Mel, on the Billings, Mont. team, faces Brooks Byrd of Roswell, N.M.

SPEAKING OF SPORTS
Strictly Personal
1966
by EARL MOREY

LAWRENCE'S GOLDEN GLOVES manager, Wesley Walker, came back from Wichita elated over his club's showing. 10 wins in 13 bouts, but deeply disappointed over the treatment given Harry Rayton, one of the better boxers in the tournament there.

The veteran Wesley feels, and many agree, that Rayton lost his chance to compete in the nationals because the Lawrence club did not take part in the recent Kansas City meet.

"But we couldn't," Wesley explains. "We have several Kansas University students on our team; it was examination time for semester grades; and it was close to the semester-break-time. Our boys would not have been ready."

Instead, Wesley, himself a former Gloves and AAU champion both as a light heavyweight and as a heavyweight. elected to enter the Wichita meet where he believes his young fighters were not given a square deal.

"Rayton had something to prove to himself, and he sure did it," Wesley explained while in his happy mood. "He whipped his man pretty good but then was not allowed to fight in the championship bout. It just wasn't right.

But there is no doubt that young Rayton is on the way up as an amateur boxer. So are several others on the squad.

★ ★ ★

"STILL, IT WAS the best showing we've ever made and I'm proud of our fighters," Wesley said. "It's a shot in the arm we needed."

There are some other things the club needs if he hopes to continue to develop championship caliber boxers. Wes's eventual goal, and one he hopes to realize in the next few years, is a Lawrence Boy's Club that would not be for boxers only. He wants a club that would appeal to a variety of interests in and out of sports. It would include the various arts and crafts, and Wesley hopes, a swimming pool.

A dinner will be held at an early date to honor the young men who did so well at Wichita. Wes hopes his good friend, Clay Hodges, outstanding West Coast amateur, will be able to attend as the featured speaker.

Hodges, a law school student from San Diego, is an AAU as well as Gloves champ, as a heavyweight.

It's been a struggle, making the Lawrence Boxing Club a going concern. Wesley feels the city is on the right track now.

★ ★ ★

SEVERAL CIVIC clubs this year joined with the Lions Club in helping carry the financial burden. KU football coach Jack Mitchell has campaigned actively for the club. So has county attorney Ralph King.

"Jack Mitchell and Ralph King have been great for our group," Wes said. "But we need others, too. We know we can't get everything we need overnight, but if we can just add a few things each year, we'll eventually have a club we can be proud of."

Walker accepts no pay for the work he does. Fact is, a lesser man would have given it up long ago. Not only has Wes had to battle for almost everything the club now has, he's had to do it the past couple of years with his left leg encased in a full-length cast. The leg he injured in that long-ago traffic accident still has not healed properly. Only recently, the dedicated guy with the quick smile underwent another operation for corrective purposes.

He doesn't look for any credit, either, and he and his boxers are thankful for any help they receive.

Frankly, even if amateur boxing isn't your cup of tea, the idea that some people are willing to give generously of their time to help others should ring a bell. Wesley Walker is one of those people and he deserves the full support of the city. I, for one, hope he gets it.

Strictly Personal

1966

When times are good and youngsters have coins jingling in their pockets, it's hard to get their minds to turn to amateur boxing. But Wesley Walker continues to try and for those who decide to give the sport a whirl, they couldn't find a better teacher or friend.

Wesley loves the ring and what it stands for. A Golden Gloves and AAU champion himself while fighting first as a light heavyweight and then a heavyweight, he retains his belief in the sport.

Walker started the Lawrence Boxing Club himself, then got backing from the Lawrence Lions Club and lately from various civic groups in the city. Two of his strongest supporters are County Attorney Ralph King and Kansas football coach Jack Mitchell.

Wes currently has eight young fighters training for the March 11-12 Golden Gloves in Wichita, and six of the eight are in the novice class.

The two hustling in the open class are lightweight Rudy Oberzan and welter weight Mike Murray. Both are potential winners.

★ ★ ★

WES WOULD HAVE entered the young men in the Kansas City Gloves, but mid-term tests at Kansas discouraged him. "We have some KU students on the team and they would not have had enough time to train," Wes explained.

But they are training now, six days a week, in the gym upstairs at 735½ N.H. St.

"We still have plenty of openings, and we still will welcome new members to the club," Wes says. All a youngster needs is the will, the courage and the stamina to train and train hard. Wesley Walker will handle the teaching part, and he will handle it well.

Walker's novice heavyweight is 225-pound Tom Dibiase, a KU soph who also doubles in football. His welterweight is Jim Fisher, and his middleweight is Hobart Woody Jr.

Another middleweight is Tony Estelle and the two light heavies in camp are Les Steckle and Stan Graham.

The club works out each evening, starting at 5:15, then at 1 p.m. on Saturdays. Anybody interested may call Wesley at UN 4-4026, or drop around the gym during workouts.

★ ★ ★

MARCH 1967

GOLDEN GLOVERS WITH AWARDS — The members of the Lawrence Boxing Club surround the trophies they won earlier in the year in the Golden Gloves in Kansas City. Shown above from left to right are John Sutton of Princeton, Kan., Chuck Cooper of Kansas City, Don Brewer, of Bellingham, Wash., Mark Brooks of Lawrence and Rudy Oberzan of Lawrence. Brewer won the 165-pound novice title. Brooks wa nner- up in the 156-pound novice class. Sutton lost his first bout in the 156-pound novice division and Cooper was beaten in his first fight in the 139-pound novice class. Oberzan lost his first bout in the 125-pound open class. The boxers were guests of the Lions Club at a dinner at the Virginia Inn this week. (Journal-World Photo)

114

Walker's Work History

Work History

High School Years--Western Construction
B.A. Green

1961--Stockley Van Camp

1963--Chemistry Department at Kansas University Chemical Storekeeper

1967--George William College, Chicago, Illinois Athletic Equipment
Manager

1979--General Motors, Broadview, Illinois 1984--US Postal Service,

River Grove, Illinois 2000--Retired General Motors as an auditor

Sport History

1962-1967--Tri-State Boxing Commission
One of 8 total in Missouri, Oklahoma, Kansas Authority to set up
Missouri AAU Boxing

Athletics History

1961-1967--Lawrence Boxing Coach
1968-1973--Wheelchair Track and Field Coach Track and Field, "Chicagoland",
Illinois

Bibliography

Bibliography

Domen, Dennis and Barbara Watkins. *Embattled Lawrence: Conflict and Community,* Lawrence, Kansas: University of Kansas Press, 2001.

Gates, Kathy Scott and Cindy Schott. *Boys, Let Me Down Easy,* Lawrence, Kansas: Allen Press, 2005.

Gordon, John Steele. *A Thread Across the Ocean: The Heroic Story of the Transatlantic Cable,* New York: Walker & Company, 2002.

Hoffman, Frederick L. *Race Traits and Tendencies of the American Negro,* New York: Macmillan Co., 1896 (for the American Economic Association.)

Jacobs, Barry. *Across the Line,* Guilford, Connecticut: Lyons Press, 2008.

Monhollon, Rusty L. *This Is America? : The Sixties in Lawrence, Kansas,* New York: Palgrave Macmillan, 2002

N.A.A.C.P. *The Crisis* (Magazine): New York: N.A.A.C.P., 1927.

Napier, Rita. *Kansas and the West: New Perspectives,* Lawrence, Kansas: The University of Kansas Press, 2003.

Packard, Jerrod M. *History of Jim Crow,* New York: St. Martin's Press, 2002

Newspapers

Lawrence Daily Journal World

(Tom Meagher 2/02/2000)
And Sport Writers 1953-1967

The Lawrence Outlook

 Staff Sport Writers

Wichita Eagle-Beacon

Joplin Globe

Las Vegas Review